CHINA AND OTHER SPACES

SELECTED ESSAYS BY CONTRIBUTORS TO THE RESEARCH
SEMINAR SERIES OF THE INSTITUTE OF COMPARATIVE
CULTURAL STUDIES AT THE UNIVERSITY OF
NOTTINGHAM NINGBO, CHINA, 2005–2007

edited by
Paul Gladston

Critical, Cultural and Communications Press
Nottingham
2009

CONTENTS

Acknowledgments

I would like to thank Bernard McGuirk, who first suggested the compilation and publication of this collection of essays, Macdonald Daly for his support with its editing, Ian Gow, the first Provost of the University of Nottingham Ningbo, for supporting the seminar series upon which this collection is based, and Nick Hewitt, without whose trust and vision none of this would have been possible.

I would also like to thank my wife Lynne and my daughter Alicia, for putting up with all of this "non-sense".

Paul Gladston

Preface

The field of comparative cultural studies has no definitive boundaries. Not only does it characteristically seek to illuminate instances of cultural difference as well as similarity but, in doing so, it also upholds the possibility, as Robert Stam suggests in the essay he has contributed to this collection, of a continuing "contrapuntal" reassessment of established cultural and academic values; one where meaning arises out of a dynamic critical interaction between differing cultural positions rather than the use of one cultural position as a foundation for the juxtapositional analysis of another. As the first in a projected series dedicated to current academic research and writing in the field of comparative cultural studies, this publication seeks to align itself with Stam's vision of contrapuntal action by presenting a highly diverse range of essays that have no single investigative theme or shared interpretative stance. The series which this volume inaugurates is not, however, envisaged simply as a serially incomplete record of the current plurality of comparative cultural research. Rather, it is also projected as having the capacity to encompass far more focused, though still interactive, responses to the comparative study of cultures both in terms of subject matter and methodological approach. Consequently, it is hoped that while this present volume points towards the insistent heterogeneity of contemporary comparative cultural research, it is also indicative of more specific lines of enquiry that might be addressed in future editions of the series.

Paul Gladston

Introduction

Paul Gladston
University of Nottingham

> [...]*the miseries of the*
> *present life, and the*
> *Barbarities of Mankind,*
> *the fatall disadvantages*
> *we are all under and the*
> *Hazard we run of being*
> *eternally Undone, lead the*
> *True Architect not to*
> *Harmony or to Rationall*
> *Beauty but to quite*
> *another Game.*[1]

As its sub-title indicates, this publication contains essays by contributors to a series of research seminars hosted by the Institute of Comparative Cultural Studies at the University of Nottingham Ningbo, China between 2005 and 2007. It therefore carries with it a certain "historical" significance insofar as it can be understood to document events during the formative development of the University of Nottingham Ningbo, China, which, in 2004, became the first jointly run Sino-foreign university to start operating within the People's Republic of China as part of the country's renewed openness to outside economic and cultural influences following on from the adoption of Deng Xiaoping's "Open-Door" policy in 1978. Beyond its role as a minor historical document, the limits of the present publication are, however, far from being clear-cut. Though it is projected as the first in a series of publications dedicated to current academic research and writing in the field of comparative cultural studies, the collection of essays which it contains has no single overarching investigative theme or premeditated focus for debate. There is, in addition, no commonly held methodological or theoretical approach that might otherwise link the conspicuously diverse array of subjects which those essays

---

[1] Peter Ackroyd, *Hawksmoor* (London: Abacus, 1991), p. 9.

cover. Consequently, there has been no attempt to structure the contents of this book according to a series of strongly related thematic headings. Instead, writings have been grouped together in a self-consciously open-ended manner on the basis of shared characteristics that were not foreseen and that have no overall consistency (indeed, not only could some essays have been placed quite easily within more than one of the chosen groupings, it would also have been possible to categorise the contents of this collection as a whole in a number of different ways). Moreover, no definitive conclusion will have been drawn here as to the collective significance of the texts at hand.

At this point it would be convenient, given the widespread climate of studied uncertainty under which academic enquiry now proceeds, to insist that the present collection of writings (if not the individual writings themselves) was intended from the outset to act as a direct form of critical intervention; one that, in a manner akin to the insistently non-linear display of artworks in the permanent collection of Tate Modern in London, knowingly appropriates accepted academic conventions only to subvert them by actively eschewing any abiding sense of thematic or narrative coherence. In actuality, however, the evident "formlessness" of this anthology was determined – as is so often the case in relation to retrospective claims of critical intent (one thinks in particular of events surrounding Marcel Duchamp's incendiary (non)-presentation of the ready-made *Fountain* in 1917) – in the first instance at least by rather more prosaic, localised and less high-minded concerns.

As previously indicated, in 2004 the University of Nottingham Ningbo, China, became the first jointly run Sino-foreign university to start operating within the People's Republic of China as part of the country's renewed openness to outside economic and cultural influences following on from the adoption of Deng Xiaoping's "Open-Door" policy in 1978. This was made possible under new legislation – first enacted in 2002 – that allows non-Chinese universities to operate in mainland China with the financial backing and administrative support of a local Chinese partner.[2]

---

[2] The University of Nottingham Ningbo, China received its first intake of students in 2004 working from premises provided for it by Wanli University in Ningbo before moving to its own purpose-built campus nearby in 2005.

Introduction

The founding aim of the University, which is situated in the rapidly growing port city of Ningbo on China's south-eastern seaboard, was to provide – within the framework of the Chinese law – an international, though predominantly Chinese, student body with undergraduate and post-graduate study opportunities directly comparable to those offered by the University of Nottingham in the UK. As a direct consequence of which, the University of Nottingham Ningbo, China sought, in close collaboration with its local partner, the Wanli Education Group, to focus its efforts from the outset not only on teaching and learning, but also on the setting up of research centres and institutes relating to key aspects of its curriculum offer; thereby, taking steps to ensure the necessary currency, relevance and international credibility of its provision.

One of the first research institutes to be established as part of this strategy was the Institute of Comparative Cultural Studies, Ningbo, which came into existence as a semi-autonomous off-shoot of the University of Nottingham's existing Institute of Comparative Cultural Studies towards the end of 2005. The initial aims of the Institute were twofold: first, to act as a focus for the research activities of its membership, which was largely made up of academic staff drawn from the University's Division of International Communications; and second, to host an annual series of research seminars showcasing the work of invited speakers in the field of comparative cultural studies that would be open to both staff and students. As might be expected, given the geographical location and the nature of the student audience, efforts were made to engage speakers from China and elsewhere whose research focused in part at least on Chinese culture. However, to avoid any undue narrowing of the Institute's scope, no special emphasis was placed on this particular area of research. The only significant guidelines set out by the Institute in relation to its research seminar series were that speakers should engage critically with the study of cultural phenomena from an openly comparative standpoint

Partly as a result of the setting of these relatively capacious boundaries, and partly because of unavoidable expediencies surrounding the engagement of international speakers in a location many regarded as attractive but remote, the range of subjects

11

addressed by contributors to the Institute's research seminar series during the first two years of its development was extremely diverse; including as it did Latin-American film, the news media in the UK and China, literatures of the supernatural, Chinese sex education, German life writing, cross-cultural communication, museology and contemporary Chinese visual art. Indeed, the investigative plurality of the series was such that for some onlookers it may well have extended the Western academy's current fascination with interdisciplinarity and internationalism almost to the point of a disastrous inarticulacy.

Nevertheless, the seminar series in question not only remained remarkably popular with both students and the University's staff – sometimes attracting audiences in the several hundreds – but also proved itself to be the focus for often refreshingly sharp intercultural as well as interdisciplinary debate; not least with regard to the questions posed by the University's overwhelmingly Chinese student body, who often maintained a high degree of (healthy) scepticism in relation to the rampant anti-foundationalism of Western academic discourse. Persistent calls for new forms of interdisciplinarity, internationalism and knowledge transfer are, of course, a common feature of contemporary academic life. However, responses to such demands – both out of the persistence of an institutional desire for academic clarity and manageability as well as the ever-present need to justify access to funding – continue to place inescapable and sometimes undue restrictions on the possibilities of discursive interaction. The research seminar series initiated by the Institute of Comparative Cultural Studies between 2005 and 2007 can therefore be understood – largely through the unusual set of circumstances within which it took place – to have engendered an uncommon (and perhaps short-lived) state of openness that, while it may often have stood at the brink of outright incoherence, also at times approached what might be seen as a highly serendipitous state of cultural interactivity and exchange. The extent to which the series entered onto the ground of either of these possibilities is, however, not something that will be assessed here with any degree of finality. Such judgements are left to those who attended the actual seminars, who will undoubtedly have their own, perhaps, differing views.

Introduction

The evident formlessness of this publication should not be seen therefore as a marker of some pre-planned critical assault on the conventions of the academic anthology. Rather, it has been maintained as a means of recounting the traces of an unusual and (as previously suggested) "historic" set of circumstances; one where researchers from very diverse backgrounds, who might otherwise have remained immured for the most part within their disciplinary boundaries, were able to present their findings within the context of a renewed Chinese internationalism, wherein an unprecedented crossing and recrossing of cultural boundaries has become a very real possibility. Even within the context of contemporary academic life where openness to cultural heterogeneity and hybridity is now something of a *sine qua non*, this text can therefore be understood to offer an insight into an uncommon series of cultural encounters many of which might not have taken place within the normal run of things.

As befits the setting, part one of this anthology contains four essays that address subjects relating to cultural encounters between China and the West. Colin Mackerras's essay, "Chinese and Western Drama Traditions: a Comparative Perspective" maps out points of departure for a comparative study of the Chinese and Western traditions of dramatic performance. In it Mackerras seeks to demonstrate that while traditional forms of Chinese dramatic performance have proceeded historically on the basis of sometimes very different concerns from those exhibited by their Western counterparts, there is nevertheless much that is shared by both; not least with regard to Western drama's continuing indebtedness to, and recently renewed fascination with, the staging of medieval and Shakespearean performance. A similar approach is taken by Michael Kelly in his contribution "Cultural Differences in Education: Europe and China". In this essay Kelly not only traces an extended genealogy of the philosophical thinking that has underpinned teaching and learning within a Western tradition, but also seeks to compare that thinking with that upon which teaching and learning in China has been conventionally based. This then enables Kelly to cast a critical eye on contemporary attitudes to education in the UK. In his essay "André Malraux and Shanghai", Nicholas Hewitt sets aside direct cultural comparison in favour of an analysis which looks towards the West's creative mis-readings of China. Taking Andre Malraux's political novel *La Condition humaine* as his starting point, Hewitt interrogates the seemingly smooth representational surface of the author's Shanghai, and in particular the city's Quartier Français, as a literary setting. Hewitt argues that not only is Malraux's Shanghai the imaginative construct of a man who had very little or no direct engagement with the city, but also that interwoven with the ostensible "realism" of his novel is an allegory of contemporaneous political events far closer to the author's European home. Andrew Cobbing's essay "Opium War and Memory: Revisiting the Battle of Zhoushan" is very much a product of the author's two year secondment as a lecturer and researcher to the University of Nottingham Ningbo, China. In it Cobbing, who is perhaps better known for his work on the history of Japan, addresses a little known aspect – in the UK at least – of the history of British colonialism; the assault on Zhoushan and the short-lived occupation of strategic territories in and around Ningbo by British forces during the eighteen-forties. Here, Cobbing shows that while this enterprise has long since been eclipsed in the British consciousness by the subsequent colonisation of Hong Kong, for mainland China it retains a formative place within the nation's official historical consciousness; one that seeks to mythologise the battle of Zhoushan as a means of reinforcing national cultural identity in the face of unsettling military defeat.

Part two of this collection, "Cinema at the Border", contains two closely related essays on cinema and national identity: Lúcia Nagib's "Panaméricas Utópicas: Entranced and Transient Nations in *I Am Cuba* and *Land in Trance*" and Armida de la Garza's "Challenging the Territorial Boundaries of the Nation: Chicanos on Mexican film in the 1990s", as well as a third by Germán Gil-Curiel entitled "Music, Literature and Cinema: A Comparative Approach to the Aesthetics of Death in *Tous les matins du monde*" which addresses the rather more metaphysical question of the transition between life and death. In her essay Nagib draws our attention to two films which take Latin American national and cultural identity as their subject matter and whose extraordinary technical virtuosity and inventiveness has, especially in the case of *I am Cuba*, until recently been scandalously overlooked. Nagib draws the conclusion that in the case of both films avant-gardist technique does not detract from the desire of the film makers to address serious political and material concerns. Rather, it allows for a powerfully creative and politically vital reworking of national and cultural identities. Armida de la Garza's essay deals similarly with film making related to Latin American national and cultural identity, in this case those of Mexico and the Mexican diaspora in North America known as Chicanos (people of Mexican descent who live and work in the US). De la Garza argues that while Mexican cinema has – against the background of globalisation – recently begun to reappraise the once suspect hybridity of the Chicano, the acceptance of their uncertain positioning as a model of national cultural identity by film makers working within a persistently conservative nation is far from being complete. In his contribution to this collection, "Music, Literature and Cinema: a comparative approach to the aesthetics of death in *Tous les matins du monde*" Germán Gil-Curiel, offers an impassioned, post-Nietzschean reading of the film in question and the book upon which it is based. According to Gil-Curiel, the film's treatment of the abyssal sublimity of death is not characterised simply by notions of finality. Instead, for Gil-Curiel, it extends the possibility of an eternal (spectral) return both in theory and in practice.

The essays in part three of this collection, "Cultural Re-Visions, Performance and Display", concentrate on a diverse range of practices brought together by their shared standing as points of focus for the rethinking of cultural perspectives. In his essay, "What (Brazilian) Cultural Studies Can Learn From Tropicália" Robert Stam looks towards the Brazilian Tropicália movement of the nineteen-sixties as a forerunner of contemporary Cultural Studies. For Stam, not only does the Tropicália movement address itself in a highly prescient manner to notions of cultural hybridity and the need to rework notions of national and cultural identity in the post-colonial era, it also does so by performatively upholding the transnational complexity of Brazil's cultural identities; on the basis of which Stam calls for a renewed contrapuntal interdisciplinarity in Brazilian Cultural Studies. Jonathan Kwan's essay, "On Late Imperial Culture: the Case of the Habsburg Monarchy" shifts our focus to another complex layering of cultural identities; those of the late Austro-Hungarian Habsburg Empire. As Kwan points out, this period of Austro-Hungarian history was one very much embroiled in a significant over-determination of differing cultural discourses. Moreover, it was one that was played out in all its complexity through the art and literature of the time. Lynne Howarth's essay, "A Cabinet of Uncertainties: the Marianne North Gallery as Hybrid Space" takes as its subject the work of the nineteenth-century British botanical illustrator Marianne North. Howarth argues that there is continuing uncertainty surrounding the function and significance of the purpose-built gallery which North commissioned to display her work at the Royal Botanical Gardens at Kew in London. Paul Gladston's essay "Inclining towards Reversion: Gu Dexin's *2007.04.14*" is the product of a direct immersion in Contemporary Chinese culture. In it Gladston addresses the emergence of increasingly essentialist readings of contemporary Chinese visual art through a close analysis of the potential significance of an installation by the Chinese artist Gu Dexin. With regard to which, he argues that the work concerned is a complex cultural hybrid of (always and already hybridised) Western and Chinese artistic thought and practice that, as a consequence, roundly problematises the application of any single interpretative point of view.

Part four, "Culture, Society and the Self" couples two essays: Roger Woods's "The Uses of East German Autobiography since the End of the GDR" and Lili Hernández's "Reviewing the Social: Bringing 'Playing' into the Everyday". In his essay Roger Woods gives a considered response to the growing body of life-writing that has emerged in eastern Germany since the fall of the Berlin Wall. While Woods accepts the importance of this writing as a sign of Germany's continuing struggle to reconcile current notions of national and cultural identity with the insistent traumas of War, Holocaust and geographical/political/economic division, he is also at pains to show how life writing in post-division Germany leads not to a clear understanding of the positioning of individual subjects in relation to this struggle, but to rather more complex and inconclusive subject positions. In her essay Hernández addresses continuing concerns with social alienation and resistance. However, she does not seek to do so simply from the point of view of an overarching political meta-narrative, but instead by the combined use of personal anecdote and various theories of "playing". What emerges is a highly personalised response – as befits current critical responses to the everyday – that nevertheless points towards the practical possibility of a wider transformative response to the life-world – a most fitting point, perhaps, upon which to conclude these introductory remarks.

CHINA AND THE WEST

Chinese and Western Drama Traditions:
a Comparative Perspective

Colin Mackerras
Griffiths University

This article aims to draw a few similarities and differences between Western and Chinese theatre traditions. This will be done in a way that tries not to cast judgements or prefer one to the other.[1] This is a vast subject and space limitations preclude this essay from being in any way comprehensive in its scope. The structure is topical, which means that period is not the focus. However, most examples will be drawn from the 15th to the 19th centuries, corresponding approximately to the eras from the Renaissance to romanticism or high imperialism in the West, and to the late imperial period in China, especially the Ming (1368-1644) and Qing (1644-1911) dynasties.

I focus on drama, which I understand as a form of theatre with three essential characteristics. These are: there is a story or plot; there are actors performing and impersonating individual characters; and there are interrelationships among the characters in the plot, even if they do not appear on stage.

This article will give no attention to such performance arts as dance, song, clowning or acrobatics unless they are within a drama or opera.

Genres of drama

Both the West and China have produced drama in many different traditions and genres. In the West there are plays from within

---

[1] In his monumental study of Chinese theatre, *The Chinese Conception of the Theatre* (Seattle and London: University of Washington Press, 1985), Hsü Tao-Ching devotes the whole of Part V (pp. 363-667) to "The Chinese and the European Theatre", especially comparisons and contrasts between the two. On p. 367 he states that "in this book no *a priori* assumption is made of the relative value of the Chinese and the European stage. They are to be compared as independent types, each existing in its own right". The present writer shares this overall assumption.

many cultures that fall today within numerous different nation states. In such plays, dialogue or monologue through speech rather than song is usually primary. The West also has a magnificent tradition of opera, which is "the generic term for musical dramatic works in which the actors sing some or all of their parts". "Opera is a union of music, drama and spectacle" and though these three "have been combined in different ways and degrees in different countries and historical periods", music normally plays a dominant role.[2] It arose at the beginning of the 17th century, which is in the first half of the period of focus here.

In China dramatic productions of the Ming and Qing belonged to the category nowadays termed *xiqu*, which literally means "song theatre". We can see the primacy of song here, and the *xiqu* item in which there was no music was extremely rare. The "spoken drama" (*huaju*), which features speech as primary, did not come into existence until the early 20th century. In *xiqu*, "performance is stylised and conventionalised, and synthesises story, music, song, speech, dance and pantomime, and frequently martial arts and acrobatics as well".[3] Clearly *xiqu* is very similar to opera, but not identical. It is variously translated as "Chinese traditional theatre", "Chinese music-drama" or "Chinese opera".[4]

The 16th century saw the development of an elite form of drama called *Kunqu* in Kunshan, Jiangsu Province, very near Shanghai, the music of which was dominated by the Chinese transverse flute, or *dizi*. *Kunqu* spawned a great many fine dramatists, but had declined drastically by the end of the 19th century. Meanwhile, a range of forms of popular regional theatre spread throughout both north and south China, spawning by the 19th century a style that is nowadays termed *jingju* and usually known by its English translation Peking Opera, "a complex art integrating song, dance, acting, mime, acrobatics, music, and

---

[2] Stanley Sadie, "Opera", in Stanley Sadie (ed.), *The New Grove Dictionary of Music and Musicians* (London: Macmillan, 1980), vol. 13, p. 544.

[3] Joel Trapido (general editor), *An International Dictionary of Theatre Language* (Westport, Connecticut, London, England: Greenwood Press, 1985), p. 962.

[4] Elizabeth Wichmann-Walczak and Trevor Hay, "*Xiqu*", in Samuel L. Leiter (ed.), *Encyclopedia of Asian Theatre* (Westport, Connecticut, London: Greenwood Press, 2007), vol. 2, p. 853.

dialogue with elaborate costumes and performance techniques".[5]

One difference between China and the West is in social status and authorship. Drama as a form held a far lower status in China than it did in the West. Apart from the aristocratic *Kunqu* mentioned above, the educated elite who determined social values regarded almost all Chinese drama of the 15th to the 19th centuries as so lowly as not really to count as literature at all. Indeed, the educated elite usually did not attend such dramas and could even be the target of social censure if they did. In the West, individual items might be condemned but the category "drama" was certainly literature and included some of the best literature of all.

In China, popular and regional theatre was actor-centred, not author-centred. Plays were based on earlier stories, novels and dramas, and we do not know the authors of the scripts of the great majority of traditional popular dramas, although those of *Kunqu* are usually known. Popular dramas were mostly not even written down and were passed orally from one generation to the next. As for the music, we cannot attribute particular composers to the popular regional dramas. Even in the case of the *Kunqu* the playwright simply selected an already known tune and assigned it to the lyrics he (there were no female playwrights in those days) had written, the composer of most of the tunes being unknown or irrelevant. Western dramas, including operas, tended to be more author- or composer-centred than in China. Of course, there is a great tradition of actors and singers, but it was the playwrights and the composers, not the performers, who carry on the mainstream of the tradition.

The purpose of drama

It is of course possible to read drama as well as perform it, provided it is written down. However, in considering the purpose of drama, I refer mainly to performance. In China, drama is more an exclusively performance art than in the West. Li Yu (*c.* 1611-80), a major playwright, theorist and man of the theatre wrote that the only reason for writing a play "is to have it performed

[5] Colin Mackerras and Elizabeth Wichmann-Walczak, "*Jingju*", in Leiter (ed.), *Encyclopedia of Asian Theatre*, vol. 1, p. 291.

onstage".[6] While many in the West would agree, there may traditionally be many people who would feel they benefit from reading drama scripts even if they do not see them on stage.

Both the West and China have shared reasons for dramatic performance. In both civilisations, ordinary people have wished to be entertained and to socialise through drama. Indeed, audiences are extremely important for performance and they may see entertainment as the primary or sometimes even only purpose of drama. Yet, elites and philosophers in both China and the West have also perceived a range of other purposes besides entertainment, which they might consider more profound.

Christians have seen the purpose of drama to worship God and encourage audiences to follow the path of rectitude. A parallel but somewhat different Confucian notion takes a more prosaic and this-worldly approach, holding the purpose of drama as promoting social harmony and good relationships, with positive characters appropriate to show on stage being "righteous men and chaste women, filial sons and obedient grandsons".

Both civilisations have on occasion wished to put forward a particular political, social or ethical message through drama. The counterpoint of such a notion is censorship, especially the wish of governments to prevent the use of drama as a means of opposing them or trying to overthrow them. In China, with its generally unified imperial system, the emperors had censors keep out an eagle eye for subversive or immoral dramas, and in 1777, the Qianlong Emperor (r.1736-96) set up a special commission to revise drama scripts so that they were in line with his Confucian moral and political standards, including that greatest of all Confucian virtues filial piety, as well as loyalty to the state and women's chastity.[7]

The fourth-century thinker Roman writer Aelius Donatus approvingly quoted Cicero to the effect that comedy is "a copy of life, a mirror of custom, a reflection of truth".[8] The image of the

---

[6] Faye Chunfang Fei (ed. and trans.), *Chinese Theories of Theater and Performance from Confucius to the Present* (Ann Arbor: The University of Michigan Press, 1999), p. 83.

[7] Colin Mackerras, "Censorship: China", in Leiter (ed.) *Encyclopedia of Asian Theatre*, vol. 1, p. 81.

[8] Barrett H. Clark (comp.), newly revised by Henry Popkin, *European*

mirror is retained by the man with as good a claim as any to be called the greatest dramatist of all time, when he has Hamlet declare that "the purpose of playing ….was and is to hold, as 'twere, the mirror up to nature; to show virtue her own feature, scorn her own image, and the very age and body of the time his form and pressure".[9] Compare that with four lines in the prologue to a farce *Roar with Songs* (*Ge dai xiao*), probably by the 16th-century Chinese playwright Xu Wei (1521-93). In somewhat less elevated and more cynical language they express a very similar point of view:

> The world is full of defects from the start,
> So is man sly and wicked deep in his heart.
> What you see and hear every day
> Are more than enough for many a new play.[10]

Plot

Naturally both in China and the West drama plots try to give play to emotions and both civilisations stress unity and coherence within the individual drama. Western dramas often follow the Ancient Greek model, a typical item seeing the problem exposed, followed by complicating factors, leading to a climax and denouement, with tension and conflict generally necessary and perhaps a surprise ending. Though most European dramas are set in Europe, there are quite a few that are not.

In terms of plot, the dramas of the Ming and Qing periods are very different from those of the West. For a start, other than mythical dramas set in such places as the Moon, all take place in China. They tend to be episodic rather than climactic. They are based on novels and stories and older dramas. There is certainly an element of surprise, complexity or crisis in many, but as one writer has expressed it, "plot structure was not a primary concern of the

---

Theories of the Drama, with a Supplement on the American Drama (New York: Crown Publishers, 1965), p. 34.
[9] *Hamlet, Prince of Denmark*, Act III, Scene A, lines 22-5. *Collins Complete Works of William Shakespeare* (Glasgow: Harper-Collins, 1994), p. 1101.
[10] See Fei (ed. and trans.), *Chinese Theories of Theater and Performance* ,p. 48.

dramatist" in traditional China.[11]

One of the most important of all subdivisions of Chinese traditional dramas is *wen* (civil) and *wu* (military). A "civil drama" concerns romance, marriage and similar topics, while a "military" drama is about battles of old times, rebellion and civil war. In a typical romance drama, a scholar courts a young lady, whose parents may not be too keen on him, but who wins his bride by passing the civil-service examinations and entering the bureaucracy. Many of the military dramas are based on the historical novel *The Romance of the Three Kingdoms* (*Sanguo yanyi*), which is about the heroes of the Three Kingdoms period (220-65). This was an actual historical era, when China was rent by civil wars. It was a blood-soaked period, but one that gave famous figures the chance to behave with courage, loyalty, patriotism and brilliance, or alternatively treachery or stupidity. Short items focusing on an episode in the Three Kingdoms are particularly common in *jingju*. Characterisation is generally fairly simple, which means that it is rare to find admirable and negative features in the same person. George Soulié de Morant is probably right in his generalisation that, whereas love frequently prevails over duty in Western drama, an excellent example being *Aida* by Giuseppe Verdi (1813-1901), what matters most in Chinese is "the merit of resistance, the proud joys of moral victory, [...] the shame and dishonour of defeat".[12]

Tragedy and comedy

One really important difference between China and the West is in the notion of tragedy. Aristotle enunciated a definition of tragedy that has exerted very profound influence over the whole of Western ideas of theatre. In Chapter 6 of his famous *Poetics* he wrote:

[11] Stephen H. West, "Drama", in William H. Nienhauser (ed. and comp.), *The Indiana Companion to Traditional Chinese Literature* (Bloomington: University of Indiana Press, 1986), p. 25.
[12] George Soulié de Morant, *Théâtre et musique modernes en Chine* (Paris: Geuthner, 1926), p. 22.

> Tragedy [...] is an imitation of a worthy or illustrious and
> perfect action, possessing magnitude, in pleasing language,
> using separately the several species of imitation in its parts, by
> men acting, and not through narration, through pity and fear
> effecting a purification from such like passion.[13]

The word here translated "purification" is *katharsis* and
unfortunately Aristotle did not develop it fully, as a result of which
there has been debate over the centuries on precisely what he
meant.[14] However, there is general consensus on the notion that
tragedy purifies the emotions in some profound way.

Another concept related to tragedy that has no real counterpart
in Chinese theatre is the tragic hero whose downfall is due to some
fault or error. Once again the source is Aristotle's *Poetics*, which
refers in Chapter 13 to the character "who neither excels in virtue
and justice, nor is changed through vice and depravity, into
misfortune, from a state of great renown and prosperity, but has
experienced this change through some error".[15] The Greek term is
harmartia, which refers to an event featuring a mistake or error,
rather than a defect in character.[16] However, again Aristotle's
precise meaning is open to interpretation and anyway not
something cast in stone in the history of drama theory. Many have
regarded the tragic hero as one who has fallen due to some fatal
flaw in character, such as Othello, brought down by jealousy.

Some Chinese dramas have an unhappy or sad ending.
However, there is in Chinese history no theory of tragedy
equivalent to the one based on Aristotle. Moreover, Chinese
commentators on traditional theatre generally believe that the
Chinese prefer the happy ending. Wang Guowei (1877-1927), the
greatest of the early modern Chinese drama critics, is an excellent
example of this, finding a reason for this preference for happy
endings in the spirit of the Chinese people:

---

[13] See Clark (comp.), *European Theories of the Drama,* p. 8.
[14] See discussion of the term *katharsis* in Jonathan Barnes, "Rhetoric and
Poetics", in Jonathan Barnes (ed.), *The Cambridge Companion to Aristotle*
(Cambridge: Cambridge University Press, 1995), pp. 277-8.
[15] Clark (comp.), *European Theories of the Drama,* p. 13.
[16] Barnes, *The Cambridge Companion to Aristotle,* pp. 279-80.

The spirit of our people is this—worldly and optimistic. Plays and novels of ancient times that exemplify this spirit are, without exception, all infused with this optimism: they begin sadly but end happily, they begin with separation but end with reunion, they begin with hardship but end with good fortune.[17]

It is obvious from this that comedy was a more familiar form of theatre in China than tragedy, even defined loosely as a drama with a sad ending. We saw earlier the importance of entertainment as a purpose of drama. Among the most important of all themes for local small-scale theatre, as well as of more developed styles like *jingju*, has always been slapstick comedy based on courting or domestic problems, with the happy ending mandatory. If tragedy is one area where difference between Western and Chinese theatre predominates over similarity, then the converse is true for comedy.

Conventions

All theatres have their conventions. Those of the period of focus in the West, from the Renaissance to the late 19th century, were a developing, expanding and diversifying panoply of immensely complex practices. The 19th-century opera may have represented an acme of these conventions, at least in the sense that the combination of spectacle and sound reached its height in the grand operas of Giuseppe Verdi and the *Gesamtkunstwerke* (total art works) or music-dramas of Richard Wagner (1813-83).

Chinese theatre was hardly static from the 15th to the 19th centuries. After all, this was when the *Kunqu* and the *jingju*, as well as the array of regional theatre styles developed. It was a period when many of the conventions of the Chinese theatre took shape while those already in existence developed, becoming more stylized and aiming towards a "harmony of effect". None of the integrated art-forms like song, speech, movement, costume and makeup could be emphasised at the expense of another.[18] The performer who could sing beautifully but whose acting skills were

---

[17] Quoted in Fei, *Chinese Theories of Theater and Performance,* p. 105.
[18] A.C. Scott, *The Classical Theatre of China* (New York: Macmillan, 1957), pp. 16-17.

less perfect or whose costuming was just a bit below par was less likely to make it in Chinese theatre than in Western opera. One very special feature of *jingju* was the highly complex and demanding but thrilling acrobatics of the military scenes, which have no real counterpart in the Western opera.

Theatres and stages

Western and Chinese theatres, including stages, have a great deal in common. In China the local temple was a frequent site for theatre, just as cathedrals were in medieval Europe and continued to be beyond the Renaissance. In China, stages were raised platforms or open spaces, some temples having permanent inbuilt stages. In these cases, the audience sat or stood in the open air, though the stage itself was covered.

In the Qing we see the rise of the big theatres, especially in Beijing. With the development of the *jingju* from the end of the 18th century came the largest kind of public theatre, which also functioned as a teahouse. These were located in the Outer City south of the Imperial Palaces. Seats were divided according to location and status, with the rich having access to much greater comfort, more space and a better view. The stage was a square thrust platform, with no front curtain, very little décor and only very simple stage properties.[19] In the Elizabethan theatre, some of the audience stood in the open air, though there were covered galleries where people could sit with a good view of the stage. As in China, the stage was of the "thrust" type, with the audience sitting on three sides. There was no curtain at the front and décor and stage properties were simple or non-existent.

The following extract gives some comment on the comparison between the Chinese theatre and Western counterparts, and especially with the Elizabethan theatre in England:

> The Chinese theatre is like the Elizabethan playhouse because the Chinese tea house is like the English inn-yard.

[19] See Colin P. Mackerras, *The Rise of the Peking Opera, 1770-1870, Social Aspects of the Theatre in Manchu China* (Oxford: Clarendon Press, 1972), pp. 197-207.

Similarly, the early Spanish theatre called *corral* (yard) had almost the same construction and origin as the Elizabethan theatre…The arrangement of the audience in the galleries, in the yard and on the stage is identical with both the Chinese temple theatre and the tea-house theatre, the fact that in the tea-house theatre all spectators on the main floor have seats and that spectators always stand on the Chinese stage are of minor importance. Pictorial reconstructions of the Elizabethan theatre often look strikingly like a Chinese theatre. In spite of the adjuncts to the Elizabethan platform stage for which are no Chinese counterparts, the stages of the two theatres are also very similar, because among the various parts of the Elizabethan stage the platform is by far the most important acting space.

A development took place in Europe in the early 17th century that was to affect theatres and theatre-going very greatly, with profound consequences that are still visible in the present day. This was the rise of the theatre with a stage topped by a proscenium arch, or simply a "proscenium stage". The first such stage was in the Teatro Farnese in Parma, Italy, which was completed in 1618. Instead of a thrust stage, the stage was like a picture frame and was dominated by a proscenium arch. Along with this development came complex décor and stage properties and the curtain at the front of the stage that could be raised or drawn aside to show the drama performance. The audience sat opposite the stage — not on three sides — and were entirely inside a theatre, with the possibility of extremely grand buildings.

Theatres with proscenium arches became widespread in England during the Restoration period in the second half of the 17th century. They coexisted throughout Europe with the older styles, becoming dominant by the 19th century. In China, the first real proscenium-stage theatre was the New Stage (*Xin wutai*), built in Shanghai in 1908. In other words, the proscenium stage was very much part of the modernisation of the Chinese theatre with the old style remaining dominant, almost to the point of being exclusive, right down to the end of the period of focus here.

[20] Hsü, *The Chinese Conception of the Theatre*, p. 464.

The social status of the actor

Let us turn now from the stage to the people who performed on it. Both in China and the West, actors have tended to hold a low social status. In both civilisations actors were seen as wanderers without fixed address who led a life of make-believe. They were often associated with the sex industry and seen as being immoral and shameless, leading people astray, especially the youth. Men of higher social status might seek sexual favours from actors, but social respect as a group was a very different matter. Actors suffered legal discrimination of various kinds. In his *La pratique du théatre* (published in 1657), François Hédélin, Abbé d'Aubignac, bemoaned the decline of the French theatre, seeing one reason in "the Infamy with which the Laws have noted those who make an open profession of being Players".[21] In China numerous laws against actors included several forbidding them or their families from sitting the civil service examinations that signalled entry into the bureaucracy and thus the cream of society.[22] In both the West and China, the rise of the "star" raised the social status at least of some actors, but in the case of China that did not even begin to happen until the late 19th century.

One interesting phenomenon is the playing of female roles by men or boys. In the theatre of the Yuan dynasty (1280-1368), women could play female roles, but in the Ming and Qing dynasties, the vast majority of troupes were exclusively male, though there were also a few that were all female, mostly prostitutes. In medieval European plays, priests or other men usually played the parts of women. It was not until the end of the 17th century that it became normal for actresses to perform female roles.[23] There were social reasons in both civilisations that made it difficult or impossible for ordinary women to go on the stage, but the implication was that impersonating women became a major skill for a certain type of male actor. Johann Wolfgang von Goethe (1749-1832), perhaps the greatest of German playwrights, exulted

---

[21] See Alois M. Nagler (ed.), *A Source Book in Theatrical History (Sources of Theatrical History)* (New York: Dover Publications, 1952), p. 177.

[22] See Mackerras, *The Rise of the Peking Opera*, pp. 40-8.

[23] See the discussion in Hsü, *The Chinese Conception of the Theatre* , pp. 620-2.

in the skills of the female impersonator. "We see a youth who has studied the idiosyncrasies of the female sex in their character and behavior; he has learned to know them, and reproduces them as artist", he wrote. "We come to understand the female sex so much the better because some one has observed and meditated on their ways".[24] Both in the West and in China, there was an association between these young actors and homosexuality.

Conclusion

One question to arise from the foregoing material is whether the differences between Chinese and Western theatres outweigh the similarities, or *vice versa*. For me, the main features of Western drama that set it apart from Chinese are in the vast developments that followed from the Aristotelian nature of tragedy and dramatic structure, and in the rise of the proscenium stage from the 17th century on. These developments implied many other changes, including an acceleration of the scale of change in the drama, the increasing complexity of *mise en scène* and the rise of the stars among actors. On the other side, Chinese drama was probably a more generally integrated art form than Western, with the various skills and arts, like song, gesture, costumes and story, locking into each other more firmly. The main similarities are in the universality of comedy, the entertainment and moral purposes of drama (though with a somewhat different set of moral values) and the whole nature of theatres and the acting profession before the 18th century. Probably the differences are more fundamental than the similarities, even if the actual number of them is no greater.

It may be possible to make an evaluation of the two drama traditions based on these similarities and differences. However, it seems to me that this would necessitate laying down careful criteria, which themselves would likely be open to question. For example, is the extent of change within a tradition more important than the degree of integration in any art-form? My personal preference is to abstain from making judgements and to accept each tradition on its own terms and applying its own criteria.

---

[24] Nagler (ed.), *A Source Book in Theatrical History,* p. 434.

Chinese and Western Drama Traditions

What is clear, however, is that the Western patterns have become accepted much more universally than the Chinese. Indeed, there is some Chinese influence on Western drama, but it is not nearly as extensive or fundamental as the other way round. In the 20th century, Chinese drama accepted Western models more comprehensively than the other way around, and many Chinese theatre-workers adopted the proscenium stage and Western drama theories.

One final question concerns survivability in the modern world. Many in China are very worried about the future of their traditional theatre. At present it is still very much alive, especially in the countryside, but does not appear to be nearly as strong as it once was. Certainly it is no longer part of the imagination of ordinary people in the way that it used to be. Some forms of theatre, especially *jingju*, have profited greatly from the burgeoning tourist industry, and there is no conceivable reason why tourists should not benefit from a national art form as much as the people that created it. But it is not clear to me that tourism can be an effective basis for the long-term strength or survivability of a set of drama forms.

How strong is Western traditional theatre? Again it appeals to tourists, and perhaps in greater numbers even than Chinese traditional theatre forms. Grand opera, Wagnerian music-drama, Shakespeare's and Molière's play can be accused of being elite forms of theatre. Yet, it seems to me that they retain an intellectual, cultural and commercial strength that probably goes beyond anything one can find in China.

For good or ill, I believe that art forms that can be associated with modernity thrive better and exert more influence in contemporary times than those that are purely traditional. Yet I do not conclude from this that traditional art-forms such as *jingju* have no future. The experience of the last few decades suggests that global forces can give rise to local. These latter often function as a kind of national popular reaction against a Western-dominated globalisation with the potential to squash individual art-forms. Certainly it is far too early to pronounce or predict the demise of China's traditional drama forms, even though they are likely to remain far more local and less global than some Western counterparts.

Photographs

The reconstructed Globe Theatre, London, taken by Colin Mackerras before an afternoon performance of *Antony and Cleopatra* in August 2006. Note the "thrust" structure of the stage. Part of the theatre is open air, as can be seen by the sun shining in.

An inbuilt temple stage in the Wuye Temple in the famous Buddhist mountain Wutai shan, Shanxi Province, taken by Colin Mackerras during a morning performance in October 2006. Note that the audience sits or stands in the open air. Audience members with seats are those who have paid for the honour of choosing the item to be performed, others watching for free.

Cultural Differences in Education: Europe and China

Michael Kelly
Southampton University

Education has always played an important role in European societies, as it has in China. There are many different approaches to education in both parts of the world, as well as broad differences between them. This paper examines some aspects of the cultural and philosophical context within which European education has developed. It suggests some of the ways in which European education might differ from the principal approaches adopted in China, and presents the most widely accepted British paradigm of education.

The context of education

When Tony Blair was asked to declare his chief political priorities during the British general election campaign of 1997, he responded "education, education, education". This became a key slogan for the government which he led.[1] He was not alone in this preoccupation, but was expressing a concern widely shared across Europe. The reasons for this priority were in the first instance economic. In particular, policy-makers emphasised the strategic importance of the "knowledge economy" in securing prosperity and in enabling Europe to compete with other parts of the world for trade and commerce. But there were also social and political reasons. Education in Europe is valued as an important component of democracy. Only if citizens can understand what is happening in the world can they make an effective contribution to discussion and decision-making. It is also valued as a factor of social inclusion, since people who lack education are less likely to be able to participate in social life and to take full advantage of opportunities. They are therefore more likely to become alienated, and in the worst case may become a danger.

These policy concerns were sufficient to place a high value on

---

[1] See Michael Fielding, *Taking Education Really Seriously: Four Years' Hard Labour* (London: Routledge Falmer, 2001), pp. xii, 260.

education. They are constantly reaffirmed in the reports and plans of governments, and in policy documents of the European institutions. To a large extent, they have been reflected in the priorities set for schools and universities, and have tended to overshadow the benefits of education for individuals. In practice, government priorities often match the motivation of learners. They expect that education will enable them to secure better careers, take more control of their own lives, and improve their standing within society. However, individuals also value education for the different kinds of personal satisfaction it gives them, enabling them to develop as people, increase their knowledge, deepen their understanding and expand their ability to enjoy life.

These reasons for regarding education as important are reflected in two distinct approaches to education that are prevalent in Europe. The first is a rationalist approach, which is instrumental in nature and oriented towards effective action. It broadly argues that the most important purpose of education is to transmit a body of knowledge and an accompanying set of values. It should foster a sense of common identity among those who are educated. And it should equip individual learners to achieve success in their future lives. The second approach is a humanistic one, which is reflective in nature and oriented towards a fuller existence. It broadly argues that the purpose of education should be to promote a love of knowledge, and an understanding of the values and processes associated with learning. It should encourage reflection on the nature of one's own identity and that of others. And it should equip individual learners to lead a satisfying life.

These competing theories have quite different conceptions of the aim and purpose of education. They appear quite antagonistic in theory, though they are not always in conflict with each other in practice. This is because they reflect the different perspectives of policy makers on the one hand, and educators on the other hand. Whereas each group has a distinct sense of its own priorities, they inevitably come to an accommodation which both groups can accept. It may even be possible to see the two approaches as complementary. Policy makers articulate a range of social expectations and set a general framework within which education can take place, including the organisation and funding of institutions and systems. Educators for their part work within this framework, complying with social expectations, but encouraging their students to adopt a wider range of aspirations. In this way, educators incorporate social requirements within a broader mission of preparation for life. The broader mission is embedded in the culture and ethos of education as it has developed over many centuries, drawing deeply on ideas and values of the European philosophical tradition.

European philosophy of education

The Western philosophical tradition began with reflection on education and many thinkers have contributed ideas and insights. Rather than attempt to condense this history, it will be useful to outline the main insights of a small number of philosophers whose work continues to inspire European ideas of education. The purpose of this is to convey the intellectual ethos within which education has developed.

Most accounts of Western philosophy take the Greek philosopher Socrates (c469-399 BCE) as a starting point.[2] He was not the first philosopher of Ancient Greece, but his reputation was established by the philosophers Plato and Aristotle, who were in some sense his students. Socrates may have been responsible for the aphorism "Know Yourself", which was engraved on the Temple of Apollo at Delphi. It certainly expresses a widely held conception that to know yourself is an important part of wisdom. Socrates was also responsible for introducing a method of inquiry based on dialogue. His approach was to question people about their ideas and beliefs, compelling them to clarify their thought and uncovering contradictions in their ideas.

The Socratic Method was adopted by some of the leading teachers in the earliest European universities, which emerged in the twelfth century. Pierre Abélard (1079-1142) was one of the most famous teachers at the University of Paris.[3] Although he is

---

[2] See Christopher Bruell, *On the Socratic Education* (New York: Rowman and Littlefield, 1999).

[3] See Constant J. Mews (ed.), *Abelard and His Legacy* (Aldershot: Ashgate, 2001); and Michael T. Clanchy, *Abelard: A Medieval Life* (Oxford: Blackwell, 1997).

better known today for the passionate lifelong relationship he had with his lover Heloïse, he made an important contribution to medieval philosophy. He introduced the method of disputation, in which two people take opposites sides on a question and debate it in public. In one of his works, called "Yes and No", he presented conflicting views from great authorities on a range of different topics. In this way, Abelard required his students to consider both sides of a question, and encouraged them to learn through argument.

The French philosopher, René Descartes (1596-1650), is usually regarded as the father of modern European philosophy.[4] He suggested that philosophy should begin from a proposition that could not be doubted. He argued that all ideas and beliefs could be cast into doubt, with the exception of the idea that we are thinking. This led him to his most famous dictum "I think therefore I am". He laid great emphasis on the need for people to think through an argument logically from first principles. His philosophy encouraged people to challenge accepted wisdom and only to believe things which have a clearly reasoned basis. In this way, he thought, we can learn through questioning received ideas and through thinking clearly.

A close contemporary, the English philosopher John Locke (1632-1704), took this a stage further, arguing that individuals are born with a fresh and open mind.[5] They develop their ideas through thinking about their experience. As a result, he argued, we should seek after truth through using our own reason, rather than accepting the opinion of authorities. We need to compare ideas we encounter, and make judgements for ourselves. He believed that we can learn best by reflecting on our experience, and by comparing our ideas to what actually happens in the world.

During the 18th century, many European countries experienced a renewal of critical thinking, which became known as the Enlightenment. One of its most influential thinkers was the Swiss writer, Jean-Jacques Rousseau (1712-1778).[6] He believed that

---

[4] See Bernard Williams, *Descartes: The Project of Pure Enquiry* (London: Routledge, 2005) pp. xviii, 308.

[5] See John W. Yolton, *John Locke and Education* (New York: Random House, 1971), p. 103.

[6] See Leslie F. Claydon, ed., *Rousseau on Education* (London: Collier-

everyone is born free but is restricted and restrained by society. He argued that this was the root cause of social problems, and that the solution was to liberate the natural goodness in people. He thought it was the task of education to encourage people to discover their inner nature and to develop their full potential. The aim of education in his view was to enable every individual to achieve personal fulfilment.

One of the most important German philosophers of the 19th century was Karl Marx (1818-1883).[7] As a leader of the labour movement, he attached great importance to the need for working people to gain education and to understand the world better. He thought that practical activity was a key part of learning, rather than merely reading books. However, he believed strongly that education was not an end in itself, but rather a means to improving life; his best known thesis states that "philosophers have only interpreted the world in various ways; the point is to change it".[8]

Another German philosopher of that period, Friedrich Nietzsche (1844-1900) took a radical view of education.[9] He was determined that the next generation of people should be superior to their predecessors. He systematically questioned received wisdom, and challenged students to find new ways of doing things. Only in this way could the human race grow in knowledge and understanding. He thought it was the role of teachers to challenge their students in this way, knowing that the students would learn more than the teachers knew. He declared that "one repays a teacher badly if one remains nothing but a pupil".[10]

Finally, the modern British philosopher, Bertrand Russell (1872-1970), argued that critical thinking was the key to

---

Macmillan, 1969), p. 147.

[7] See David McLellan, *Karl Marx: His Life and Thought* (London: Macmillan, 1973); and Andrew Collier, *Marx* (Oxford: Oneworld, 2004) pp. vi, 170.

[8] This is included in the XIth Thesis on Feuerbach, and is quoted in most anthologies, such as Karl Marx, and Friedrich Engels, *Marx/Engels Selected Works, Volume One* (Moscow: Progress Publishers, 1969).

[9] See David E. Cooper, *Authenticity and Learning: Nietzsche's Educational Philosophy* (London: Routledge and Kegan Paul, 1983).

[10] See Friedrich Wilhelm Nietzsche, *Thus Spoke Zarathustra: A Book for Everyone and No One* (Harmondsworth: Penguin, 1969), p. 343.

education.[11] He developed an analytical approach to philosophy, greatly informed by mathematics, and applied it to many social and political issues. He perceived that a lack of clear thinking contributed to most of the world's problems, and is often quoted as saying, "Many people would sooner die than think. In fact they do."[12] He argued that established views should be challenged and that through a process of criticism, people could learn to think clearly. They would then be able to take effective steps to improve things.

Comparing European and Chinese conceptions

From this brief characterisation of European thinking, it is clear that there are many points of contact with Chinese philosophers who have written about education from the time of Confucius (Kong Fuzi, c.551-479 BC) and Mencius (Meng Zi, c.372-289 BCE).[13] The importance of thinking and studying is a theme common to the European and Chinese traditions. The emphasis on practical application is also common to traditions. Both frequently recommend that students should learn by doing, should put into practice the things they have learned, and should pay attention to someone who is proficient at doing what they wish to learn. In modern terms, this is usually expressed as work-based learning, and suggests a close link between the classroom and the workplace.

Perhaps the most striking difference between the traditions is the role assigned to the teacher. In the Chinese tradition, there is an expectation of high respect for the teacher and obedience to him or her. This is clearly related to the cultural value placed on the authority of parents and wise adults. By contrast, the European

[11] See Caroline Moorehead, *Bertrand Russell: A Life* (London: Sinclair-Stevenson, 1992).

[12] Quoted in Antony Flew, *Thinking About Thinking : Or, Do I Sincerely Want to Be Right?* (London: Fontana-Collins, 1975).

[13] See Jingpan Chen, *Confucius as a Teacher* (Beijing: Foreign Languages Press, 1990). For the following discussion I am grateful to the students at the University of Nottingham-Ningbo, who contributed their perceptions of Chinese attitudes to education.

tradition is to encourage students to question their teachers, and to become increasingly independent of them. This is no doubt linked to the cultural value placed on youth in European societies. A second difference lies in the attitude to inherited knowledge and wisdom. The Chinese tradition lays strong emphasis on transmitting established knowledge and a body of cultural values important to the cohesion of society. This is not unlike the rationalist view of education, outlined above. But it is different from the humanist view, which emphasises the need to challenge received wisdom. This view also emphasises the importance of understanding general principles rather than building up a body of knowledge.

These similarities and differences are related to underlying cultural attitudes and values, which apply to many aspects of life. It is useful to compare them by using the measures of culture developed by the Dutch sociologist, Geert Hofstede.[14] He proposed five "cultural dimensions" which enabled him to draw a profile of the cultural values and attitudes most widely held by people in particular countries. His research suggests that there are three dimensions on which British and Chinese cultural attitudes are significantly different.[15]

The most striking difference is in what Hofstede terms "long-term orientation". Chinese participants in his studies place a very high value on the long term. They are prepared to persevere for a long time, showing patience, and valuing harmony in relations of cooperation. British participants, on the other hand, show a more short-term orientation. They are concerned to establish the truth, anxious to achieve results rapidly, and willing to change their approach if it proves unsuccessful.

A second difference lies in the dimension of individualism and collectivism. In this area, Chinese participants show a strong attachment to their family, friends and networks, with whom they have close relationships. They are willing to sacrifice themselves for the greater good of the group and take responsibility for others. British participants, by contrast place a high value on the

---

[14] See Geert Hofstede, *Culture's Consequences. International Differences in Work-Related Values* (London: Sage, 1980).
[15] Recent studies of this are presented on Hofstede's website:
http://www.geert-hofstede.com/geert_hofstede_resources.shtml

rights of individuals, and the need for people to take responsibility for their own lives. They have extensive networks of friends and acquaintances, with whom they maintain looser relationships.

The third significant difference is in what Hofstede call the "power-distance ratio". This is a measure of the extent to which people accept and expect inequality of power within society. Chinese participants place a high value on respect for authority. They expect to mark the differences of power in clear ways that enable everyone to understand clearly what their own rank and status is in relation to others. British participants, on the contrary, have a strong attachment to independence of mind. The have a sense of the fundamental equality of people, and value their ability to establish relations of mutual respect across differences of rank and status.

In each of these three dimensions, British and Chinese cultural attitudes are noticeably different, though examples of all of these attitudes can be found in both countries, and are in various ways valued. Both countries also appear to have very similar profiles in relation to Hofstede's other cultural dimensions, which assess the "masculinity" of a society and its ability to tolerate uncertainty. They provide a context within which the British approach to education appears to be distinctive, and in some respect different from the prevailing approach in China.

British paradigm of education

In the past ten years, higher education in Britain has been the focus of a great deal of policy making from government, and a great deal of research by educationalists. The result has been the emergence of a consensus on the nature of education, which provides a paradigm widely accepted by universities.[16] To a large

---

[16] See, for example: Heather Fry, Steve Ketteridge, and Stephanie Marshall (eds.), *A Handbook for Teaching and Learning in Higher Education: Enhancing Academic Practice* (2nd ed., London: Kogan Page, 2002); Greg Light, and Roy Cox, *Learning and Teaching in Higher Education: The Reflective Professional* (London: Paul Chapman, 2001); Gill Nicholls, *Developing Teaching and Learning in Higher Education* (London: Routledge-Falmer, 2002); Eric Sotto, *When Teaching Becomes Learning: A Theory and Practice of*

extent the concept of "education" has been replaced by the concept of "learning and teaching". The effect of this shift has been to focus on the institutions involved, and to emphasise the systems and processes that need to be put in place in order to achieve clearly defined outcomes. This has both benefits and drawbacks when compared with the older notion, which presents education as a broader, more holistic activity. On the one hand, it has the benefit of enabling pedagogical processes to be examined and improved. On the other hand it has the disadvantage of segregating pedagogy from the broader social context of education. In other words, it proposes an analytical approach, which is very powerful, but at the expense a synthesis in which all the dimensions of education are drawn together.

The most important innovation in the paradigm is to shift the focus from the teacher to the learner. The purpose of education is to produce learning, and its value is measured by the success of learners in developing their knowledge and skills. In this perspective, teaching is just one of several resources that learners can draw on. The role of teachers is judged by how effective they are in enabling students to learn. This approach is set in the wider context of "lifelong learning", a concept that has become popular in Europe over the last decade. Lifelong learning involves recognition that the learning achieved in formal education will not be sufficient to last through the learner's life. On the contrary, there is an understanding that the world is changing rapidly, and that people will constantly need to learn new things throughout their lives. However, it will be the responsibility to individuals to identify their learning needs. They will not be able to rely on the formal education system to provide the learning they will need, but will have to find the learning opportunities themselves. Consequently, it is important in formal education that students should learn how to learn. That is, they must pay attention to such issues as how to identify their own learning needs, their own learning style and the kinds of strategy they should adopt in order to achieve their learning requirements. The result of this has been to encourage the adoption of "student-centred education". In practice, this means not only putting students at the centre of the

---

Teaching (2nd ed.; New York: Continuum International, 2007).

learning process but also ensuring that the accompanying support services and facilities are tailored to meet the requirements of students. Increasingly, this also means finding increasingly flexible ways of enabling students to learn, rather than expecting them to comply with a closely structured system.

The goal of student-centred learning is to develop the learner's independence as far as possible, making students responsible for their own learning and equipping them with the means to learn on their own. It is expected that teachers will provide advice and guidance so that students are not simply left to fend for themselves, but are helped to acquire the knowledge and skills they need to work independently. As they develop greater autonomy, students will come to see teachers as a resource among others, and will expect to discuss a wide range of issues with them. Teachers are expected to be well informed on the subject they are studying, but they also advise students on methods of enquiry that will help them to discover new knowledge. Increasing recognition is now given to the importance of a "learning community", in which a number of people cooperate to develop their learning. While teachers are a part of this, the role of other students is recognised as being important, as students discuss questions with other students, and help each other with their learning.

Within this paradigm, the role of the teacher is therefore different from the traditional role as custodian of knowledge and figure of authority. Teachers are not mainly required to transmit the knowledge they themselves have accumulated. Their role is to support and motivate learners, inspiring them with a desire for knowledge. They also provide resources that the students will need in order to learn. Their role is to be available to students to discuss issues with them, and to be a part of the learning community. It is a consequence of this that teachers expect to learn from their students. Above all, the teacher is a "reflective practitioner", who constantly thinks about how they are approaching their role and is prepared to be self-critical in order to learn and improve.

The role of the student carries correspondingly greater responsibility. They are expected to challenge existing knowledge and to question their teachers. Only by doing so can they (and their teachers) be sure that they have understood what they are studying. Rather than simply repeating what they have heard or read, they must be prepared to take risks and to experiment with ideas. Universities are a relatively safe environment in which they can do this. If they make errors, they can quickly abandon them without damage to their reputation, and can use the opportunity to try out new ways of thinking, to which they will not ultimately be bound. In this way they may produce new knowledge, or new insights and interpretations that draw on the range of knowledge and skills they have acquired. They will certainly develop a more sophisticated understanding of the world, and a clearer sense of their own beliefs and values.

Conclusion

The British paradigm discussed here is different from the prevailing paradigms in China. It is also different from the classical paradigms that have been accepted in Britain. It is widely accepted among educators though not by all. It is often contested by politicians, who would prefer a more prescriptive approach to education, where learning would be directed explicitly to fulfil particular policy objectives. The views of politicians are listened to, but even if their views were unanimous, which is far from being the case, the time cycles of politicians are shorter than those of educators. Policies often change before the corresponding measures have been introduced in the education system. In that context the British paradigm expresses the set of underlying values which continue to guide educators in the UK, and which guide the creative responses they make to the requirements of policy. They act as the compass which enables them to keep their bearing in the uncertain tides and currents of political and social change.

La Condition humaine:
André Malraux's Imaginary Shanghai

Nicholas Hewitt
University of Nottingham

In 1933, André Malraux, already one of France's best-known young writers, won the Prix Goncourt for his novel *La Condition humaine*, set in Shanghai in 1927. The novel had a considerable success, due not only to its powerful blend of the political and the metaphysical, but especially because of its authority as what was perceived as a semi-documentary work on the events in Shanghai in April 1927, with all the apparent prestige of an eye-witness account. In reality, however, Malraux had only paid a fleeting visit to Shanghai; and that as late as 1931 when the novel was already well advanced and when the events he depicts were long past. As Jean Lacouture comments:

> He took few notes in Shanghai. *La Condition humaine* was already taking shape, but he wanted to make it a metaphysical novel and the city would play no more part in it than St Petersburg in *Crime and Punishment*.[1]

In other words, as in the case of Dostoievsky, the cityscape is designed merely as a backdrop for the essentially metaphysical action which dominates and which it reflects: Malraux's Shanghai, even more than Dostoievsky's St Petersburg, which the author at least knew well, is an imaginary or imagined city, whose proper role is as the context for a poetic tragedy; nevertheless, neither the city nor the events which took place there in 1927 can be excluded entirely from a discussion of the novel. In particular, the imagined Shanghai of André Malraux is highly revealing of French, European and Western perceptions of the East in the interwar years and of their cultural and political preoccupations. In this respect, *La Condition humaine* is a late, but symptomatic, example of Edward Saïd's "Orientalism".

[1] Jean Lacouture, *André Malraux, une vie dans le siècle* (Paris: Seuil, 1973), p. 142.

Although Malraux's experience of Shanghai, and China in general, had been limited before the publication of the novel, his knowledge of South-East Asia was much deeper. A passionate amateur student of oriental art, he had made a famous journey to Cambodia in 1923 in the course of which he was arrested and charged with stealing artifacts from the temple of Banteai-Srey. In 1925 he returned to Saigon, where, with the lawyer Paul Monin, he founded an anti-government newspaper, *L'Indochine*. It was in the course of this brief anti-colonial adventure that Malraux was made a member of the Kuomintang and carried out a flying visit to Hong Kong. According to Clara Malraux, the British captain of the boat taking them from Saigon radioed Hong Kong with the news that he had on board "the reddest bolchevik [sic] of all Annam".[2] This was to be his only direct experience of China until the visit of 1931.

This early experience of the East contained two important factors which were to characterise his work up to the Second World War, and, in the case of the former, throughout his life: a fascination with Oriental art and, more generally, comparative cultural anthropology, expressed at its most extensive in the post-war *Les Voix du silence*; and an early commitment to anti-colonialism which was to take him to radical politics and a close relationship with Communism. These two inter-linked elements were represented in his early essay, of 1926, *La Tentation de l'Occident*,[3] in which, using the epistolary format derived from Montesquieu's *Les Lettres persanes*, he recounts the contrasting impressions of a Chinese traveller, Ling, in Europe, and of a Westerner, A.D., in China. What is interesting about the essay, however, is that, like Montesquieu's original work, the focus is less on the particularities of the East and more on the establishment of a cultural critique the post-First World War West. In this context, *La Tentation de l'Occident* forms part of a general European cultural self-critique deriving essentially from Nietzsche and manifesting itself in works such as Spengler's *The Decline of the West* and, in France, Valéry's "La Crise de l'esprit", and looks forward to the

---

[2] Clara Malraux, *Le Bruit de nos pas, III: Les Combats et les jeux* (Paris: Grasset, 1969), pp. 214-5.

[3] André Malraux, *La Tentation de l'Occident* (Paris: Grasset, 1926).

essentially European-centred *La Condition humaine*. At the same time, this reflection on the fallibility of Western thought and psychology served as the basis for Malraux's early fiction. *La Voie Royale*, published in 1930, but probably his first novel, is a transposition of his earlier adventures in Cambodia, in which the protagonist Claude Vannec, a young Western intellectual who has discovered the bankruptcy of his own civilisation, seeks a solution through travel and adventure, guided by the heroic man of action, Perken. In *Les Conquérants*, of 1928, that man of action becomes loosely attached to a revolutionary cause. The novel is set in the Kuomintang republic of Canton in 1925, in which the Communists, led by the Westerner Pierre Garine, jockey for position within the Kuomintang against Nationalists and Chinese traditionalists. What is interesting about the novel is that, like *La Condition humaine*, it depicts an imagined city, the Canton which Malraux was not to visit until 1931, three years after the publication, and that it celebrates the conquest and consolidation of revolutionary Communist power, but under Western leadership and with a resolutely Western focus.

La Condition humaine, published five years later, takes up the story where *Les Conquérants* left off. Set in Shanghai in April 1927, it depicts the culmination of the power struggle between Communists and Nationalists within the Kuomintang, when the Communists are eliminated by Chiang Kai Shek's Nationalists, aided by the Western powers, represented particularly by Chiang's police-chief, Matial, and the French head of the Consortium Franco-Asiatique, Ferral. Whilst the depiction of Westerners in this context is both realistic and logical, it is more surprising to see Malraux's Communist revolutionaries being led by figures who are either Western or have Western antecedents: the Russian Katow and the mixed-nationality Kyo Gisors, who has a German wife, May. Even the group's anarchist-leaning activist, Tchen, has been brought up by a Christian missionary. While the Kuomintang in general, and the Chinese Communists in particular, were indeed advised by Soviet Comintern officials, such as the factual Borodine, who also figures in *Les Conquérants*, and the fictional Vologuine, Malraux's concentration on Western or Westernised figures in the Chinese Communist struggle points clearly to a preoccupation with exclusively European values. Indeed, the very concept of "La Condition humaine" ("Man's Fate", or "Man's Estate") is derived from Montaigne's "l'humaine condition" and is an entirely Western construct. For similar reasons, one of the most powerful characters in the novel, Le Baron de Clappique, a representative of international Bohemia, is an essay in the exploration of an exclusively European temptation of self-elimination and non-existence.

Within this thematic context, it is hardly surprising that, as Lacouture records, Malraux should have shown so little interest in the reality of Shanghai itself during his 1931 visit and that he had already amassed sufficient details to act as a convincing backdrop to the essentially Western political and metaphysical action. His imaginary/imagined Shanghai is entirely conventional, designed to give the impression of authenticity and it uses a familiar common currency of description of the city in the pre-Communist period, to be found in films such as Von Sternberg's *Shanghai Express* and *The Shanghai Gesture*, or fiction such as Paul Morand's short stories in *Ouvert la nuit* and *Fermé la nuit*, Somerset Maugham's *The Painted Veil*, and Vicki Baum's *Bombs on Shanghai*. The common denominator is the corrupt and scandalous world of the Western expatriates who had turned Shanghai into "the Whore of the East" and who were located in the French and International Concessions, the Western cities within a city and under autonomous Western rule. The cosmopolitanism of Shanghai in the interwar years may, as Wu Liang suggests, have often been exaggerated,[4] but the legend of the Westernised city is certainly grounded in fact:

> There were all sorts of people living in Shanghai. Many of them took the city as their second home. There were Jewish millionaires, big-shots from Ningbo, Indian policemen, English managers, Guandong chefs, refugees from Huaibei, French attachés, writers from Sichuan, Japanese performers and Russians.[5]

[4] Wu Liang, *Old Shanghai. A Lost Age* (Shanghai: Foreign Languages Press, 2001), p. 69.
[5] Wu, *Old Shanghai*, p. 129.

The French Concession dated from the Lagrené mission of 1844, which gave to France the right to establish trading centres in Canton, Amoy, Fuzhou, Ningbo and Shanghai itself (*Le Paris de l'Orient*). In 1849, the French in Shanghai were allocated an official residential area, "situated to the North of the Chinese city" and "bounded to the East by the Huangpu and to the North by the British Concession, separated by a canal, the Yangjingbang",[6] and in 1861 set up their own independent municipal council, "under the direct authority of the Consul and therefore of the Quai d'Orsay".[7] Although initially smaller than its British counterpart (later amalgamated with the American Concession to make the "International Concession"), the French Concession grew rapidly from a modest 66 hectares in 1849 to 1000 hectares by 1914,[8] making it the "largest French city in the world",[9] the "Paris of the East". This rapid expansion of the French Concession was accompanied by an erosion of the old city structure and the creation of new roads "laid out on the lines of the North-South and East-West axes" (*Le Paris de l'Orient*) and often built on the site of old canals and water courses. The most radical, and symbolic, transformation of the old city came in 1912, with the demolition of the city walls and their replacement to the East by a boulevard separating the French Concession from the Chinese city, the Avenue des Deux Républiques, which later became the Avenue Joffre.[10] It was this city, with its banks, trading companies and financial houses on the Bund and the gambling, opium and prostitution which earned it the title of "the biggest brothel in the world" which serves as the context for Malraux's political tragedy in *La Condition humaine*.[11]

Malraux's depiction of Shanghai, as we have seen, is essentially based on second-hand material which was already in the public domain through maps, guidebooks, postcards and newspaper reports. Nor is it designed to give more than an aura of plausibility and authenticity to the events being described. *La Condition*

6 Wu, *Old Shanghai*, p. 129.

7 Wu, *Old Shanghai*, p. 129.

8 Wu, *Old Shanghai*, p. 129.

9 *Wikipédia* (http:fr.wikipedia.org/wiki/Shanghai).

10 *Wikipédia* (http:fr.wikipedia.org/wiki/Shanghai).

11 *Wikipédia* (http:fr.wikipedia.org/wiki/Shanghai).

humaine, for all the universalist preoccupations embodied in its title, is set almost entirely in the French Concession, apart from the expedition made by Kyo and Katow to see the Soviet advisor Vologuine in Hangkow, and Shanghai is evoked initially in almost conventional terms as "the largest city in China",[12] characterised by its mysterious noises, "sounds coming from the depths of the Earth".[13] In this context, the Avenue des Deux Républiques plays a crucial role as the frontier between the French Concession and the Chinese city, a frontier which Malraux and his characters rarely cross. After the murder of the Nationalist arms-dealer, for example, Tchen approaches "the Avenue des Deux-Républiques, the frontier of the Chinese city".[14]

This frontier is carefully guarded. As Tchen approaches, he notices, "at the end of the street the machine guns, almost as grey as the puddles, the flash of the bayonets carried by silent shadows: the police station, the end of the French Concession. The taxi didn't go any further…"[15] Similarly, when Kyo Gisors returns from the Chinese city, "he finally reached the fences of the concessions. Two Indochinese infantrymen and a sergeant in the colonial army came to inspect his papers."[16] Indeed, the entire Concession is under strict police control: the same evening as Tchen's murder of the arms dealer, Ferral visits the "vast buildings of the French police".[17]

The reason for this strong police presence is clear enough: France's commercial interests in Shanghai protected by the Consulate and the Municipal Council.[18] When the Communists

---

[12] André Malraux, *La Condition humaine*, in André Malraux, *Romans: Les Congérants, La Condition Humaine, L'Espoir* (Paris: Gallimard, coll. "Bibliothèque de la Pléïade", 1947), p. 186.

[13] Malraux, *Romans*, p. 186.

[14] Malraux, *Romans*, p. 186.

[15] Malraux *Romans*, p. 186.

[16] Malraux *Romans*, p. 195.

[17] Malraux *Romans*, p. 237.

[18] At the time of the events depicted in *La Condition humaine*, the French Consul in Shanghai was Paul-Emile Naggiar, who served from November 1925 to December 1927. See *Le Paris de l'Orient- Le Paris de l'Orient: Présence Française à Shanghaï, 1849-1946* (Paris: Musée Albert-Kahn and Ministère des Affaires Etrangères, 2002).

plan their attack on the arms vessel, they note that it is moored "opposite the French Consulate".[19] Ferral himself, who harbours immense political ambitions for when he returns to France, is both "President of the French Chamber of Commerce"[20] and Director of the powerful, and fictitious, "Consortium Franco-Asiatique". With a nice eye for detail, Malraux notes that Ferral's car is a Voisin, "because the President of the French Chamber of Commerce could not use an American car".[21] This commercial and political activity is concentrated on the Bund, the "Quais", which Malaux uses as recurrently as the Avenue des Deux-Répubiques in order to maintain his geographical coordinates, although, as early critics pointed out, he locates Shanghai erroneously on the Yang-Tsé instead of the Huangpo.[22]

If some of the political and commercial detail of the novel is less familiar to readers in the 1930s, *La Condition humaine* rejoins more popular and conventional depictions of Shanghai in its evocation of the world of the expatriates, located in the city's numerous pleasure-centres. Of these, the most important are the "grand hotels of the Concessions",[23] of which Malraux chooses one of the most important, the Astor, where Ferral's mistress, Valérie, lives and where she humiliates him "at the cocktail hour", when "everyone in Shanghai was there".[24] Less grand is the "petit Hôtel Grosvenor",[25] where the Baron de Clappique meets one of his seedy associates, the former Polish army officer, Count Chpilewski. Clappique himself is reduced to staying in a Chinese hotel.[26] At the same time, the expatriate community, or at least the most fortunate of them, socialise in the Cercle Français[27] and the Shanghai-Club, on the Bund, where, at the cocktail hour, "nearly everyone went to drink and meet each other".[28] Catering for more

---

[19] Malraux, *Romans,* p. 218.
[20] Malraux, *Romans,* p. 235.
[21] Malraux, *Romans,* p. 235.
[22] Malraux, *Romans,* p. 230.
[23] Malraux, *Romans,* p. 237.
[24] Malraux, *Romans,*.p. 339.
[25] Malraux, *Romans,* p. 297.
[26] Malraux, *Romans,* p. 371.
[27] Malraux, *Romans,* p. 345.
[28] Malraux, *Romans,* p. 300.

louche tastes are the night-clubs, like the Black Cat,[29] which probably owes its name to the famous Montmatre cabaret of the 1880s, Le Chat Noir, and the unnamed "maison de jeu",[30] in which Clappique whiles away the night and forgets to warn his revolutionary friends of their impending arrest. Nor does Malraux ignore the city's reputation for prostitution, although he chooses to introduce it in an oblique way: Ferral, still smarting from his humiliation by Valérie, picks up a courtesan on the Nankin Road,[31] but humiliates her in her turn by treating her as a common prostitute and not a high-class, traditional entertainer.

In fact, as we have seen, Malraux's depiction of Shanghai contains very little which could not have obtained from postcards, maps and news reports. Indeed, when Ferral, at one point, "looks at a map of Shanghai on the wall, with big red marks indicating the masses of workers and the poor",[32] he is, in a sense, replicating the work already undertaken by the author. The only exceptions are rare snippets of more detailed information, often introduced in the manner of footnotes, and which are designed to enhance the novel's documentary credentials. In the course of the fighting and the troop movements, there are more precise geographical references, to the Gare du Nord,[33] the Gare du Sud,[34] and its proximity to the barracks,[35] and the Gare de Chapei.[36] The headquarters of Chiang Kai Shek's police chief, Martial, is situated in a typical villa in the French Concession, reminiscent of those to be found in seaside resorts or the suburbs, and which Malraux characterises as "in the Bécon-les-Bruyères style".[37] Finally, in describing an attempt to assassinate Chiang as his car drives past, Malraux notes that "the custom, in Shanghai, is to drive on the left".[38]

[29] Malraux, *Romans*, p. 322.
[30] Malraux, *Romans*, p. 356.
[31] Malraux, *Romans*, p. 351.
[32] Malraux, *Romans*, p. 335.
[33] Malraux, *Romans*, p. 251.
[34] Malraux, *Romans*, p. 252.
[35] Malraux, *Romans*, p. 256.
[36] Malraux, *Romans*, p. 400.
[37] Malraux, *Romans*, p. 376.
[38] Malraux, *Romans*, p. 309.

What these and other details do is to demonstrate the ability of a relatively small number of often conventional images to create an imagined city which is capable of being as potent as the real. In this context, it is important to emphasise the highly visual quality of Malraux's literary imagination which will lead him shortly after *La Condition humaine* to the formulation of the concept of "the imaginary museum". Not merely do a number of images in the novel appear to be derived from visual material such as postcards and news photographs, they also derive, as does much of the narration, from Malraux's interest in cinema, especially the work of Eisenstein, who, incidentally, returned the compliment by beginning to plan a film of the novel.

In fact, Malraux's imagined Shanghai has two purposes. On the one hand, it is a shadowy, sometimes clichéd, Eastern city with all the hallmarks of Western Orientalism: exoticism, eroticism, but essentially lacking much in the way of detail and specificity. In this context, *La Condition humaine* looks both towards the depiction of Shanghai in the popular culture of the period, and towards the Western-centred cultural preoccupations of essays like *La Tentation de l'Occident*. At the same time, the novel clearly constructs a paradigm for revolutionary Western politics in the 1920s and 1930s. In its evocation of the massacre of the Shanghai communists in April, 1927, the novel depicts the tactical failure of the early CCP (Chinese Communist Party) in their relations with Chiang Kai Shek's Nationalists in continuing to work within what had become a redundant political union, the Kuomintang. More importantly, however, the novel apportions responsibility less to the young and relatively inexperienced CCP than to the Soviet advisors in China, and, beyond them, the Soviet leadership itself. It is probably for this reason that, in his political depiction, Malraux chooses to omit the role of the well-known alliance between the Nationalists and organised crime, in particular the "Green Gang" and concentrates on the dilemma faced by the Chinese communists in their struggle against the Nationalists and their Western capitalist colonialist allies.

In other words, *La Condition humaine* is as much about Europe in the early 1930s as it is about China in the 1920s, and Malraux's preoccupation is as much with Berlin as it is with Shanghai. The novel, after all, coincides with the electoral defeat and subsequent elimination of the most powerful Communist party in Western Europe, the German Communists, and implicitly questions the strategic wisdom of the Comintern and its ability to effectively combat the Fascist surge. For this reason, it is highly fitting that Malraux, who became one of the leaders of European intellectual anti-Fascism, should situate his next novel, *Le Temps du mépris, of 1935*, in Nazi Germany.

Opium War and Memory:
Revisiting the Battle of Zhoushan

Andrew Cobbing
University of Nottingham

In June 2006 a group of British soldiers embarked on a journey to China, their mission to find the site of a battle in which their regiment had once taken part. This was the Battle of "Chusan Heights" fought on 1 October 1841, one of the key encounters in what is commonly called the Opium War. Their experience and the opportunity this brought to review current efforts to recall the event illustrate some of the forces at play in constructing the memory of war, particularly devices and motifs used by subsequent generations to interpret what they believe occurred on a day now lost in the past. This case study revisits the battle on Zhoushan Island to explore some of the questions that arise when two parallel discourses, developed in relative isolation, are brought together for comparison 165 years after the event.

First of all, the battle itself needs to be placed in some context by taking into account the strategic importance of Zhoushan and its role in the Opium War. Background is also required on the Westmoreland Regiment, its connection with China, and "Exercise Global Dragon", the project which resulted in these four soldiers making the trip to Zhoushan in 2006. This is to help clarify their motives for visiting the site of the event their regiment remembers as the Battle of "Chusan Heights". Relating their experience there also illustrates one example of how and why different communities embark on the process of acquiring, if not reclaiming, a sense of meaning from key dates in their past.

Zhoushan in the Opium War

The Zhoushan archipelago, China's largest, is situated off the coast of Zhejiang Province and consists of 1,339 islands in all stretching a considerable distance into the East China Sea. To outsiders the area is best known for the small island of Putuo-shan, a sacred

Buddhist centre that has become a popular tourist attraction. A ferry trip from the mainland, however, soon reveals how much the local economy depends on fishing, with thousands of small boats to be seen at work. These islands are the richest fishing grounds off China's coasts, and seafood features prominently not only locally but also in the cuisine of Ningbo, the nearest major city on the mainland.

Other features visible on approaching the main island include naval vessels of the People's Liberation Army (PLA). Zhoushan guards the approach to Hangzhou Bay from the south, also Shanghai and the mouth of the Yangtze River. Not only approachable from the sea, the islands afford access to the populous and prosperous heartland of China. This was why in medieval times the Zhoushan archipelago was exploited as an operational base by Japanese pirates (*wokou*). From here they marauded along the coast, and for long periods the main island, too, was under *wokou* control. More recently, when Mao Zedong proclaimed the Communist state on 1 October 1949, Zhoushan was still occupied by Chiang Kai-shek's Guomingdang forces and was not secured until the following year. Today, therefore, it remains an important strategic base, and both army and navy facilities are very much in evidence in Dinghai, the main city, including a sizeable naval shipyard. This is China's frontier in the East China Sea, a region of contested waters shared with Taiwan, Japan and Korea.

It was due to this strategic importance that Zhoushan featured prominently in the Opium War. The immediate cause of the conflict may have been trade friction far to the south in Canton, but from the outset the British were aware that their steamships and firepower offered them a technological advantage which could threaten the heartland of China's political control, if only they could gain a foothold in Zhoushan. During the war British forces attacked and occupied the main island twice – in 1840 and again in 1841. On both occasions their target was Dinghai, then a walled city situated half a mile inland.

First of all, in 1840 a British fleet moved north along the Chinese seaboard aiming straight for Zhoushan. It was a daring strategy that came as a complete surprise to Commissioner Li, Commander-in-Chief of the Chinese forces, who had concentrated his defences around Canton. A small garrison of 2,000 men was guarding Dinghai when the fleet arrived. The equally surprised islanders told the invaders that "if the British had complaints about Canton, they should go and fight the Cantonese, not make Zhoushan suffer".[1] Nevertheless, on 6 July the city of Dinghai was seized and the island secured. It was the first territory that the British ever occupied in China.

Although Zhoushan had been captured without much difficulty, the British garrison stationed there was soon ravaged by disease, notably malaria, reducing its strength by a third before the year was out. By this time part of the British fleet had pushed north as far as the mouth of the Bei River, within striking distance of Beijing and close enough to the imperial court to force the Manchu authorities to negotiate terms. The outcome was the Convention of Chuenbi signed on 20 January 1841, whereby Zhoushan was exchanged for control of Hong Kong. A few days later British troops occupied Hong Kong, and the following month the garrison in Dinghai duly evacuated. The peace was only temporary, however, for back in London Foreign Secretary Lord Palmerston was furious that Zhoushan, which he saw as an advantageous location for trade, had been surrendered in return for "the barren island of Hong Kong".[2] The Emperor, too, was indignant at this loss of territory, and renewed military preparations were soon underway to drive the British out.

In Zhoushan, for example, concerted efforts were made to protect the city of Dinghai from further attack. Reinforcements arrived from the mainland, including detachments of Manchu warriors, and before long a formidable garrison of 5,800 soldiers was based on site.[3] Defensive walls were built along the seafront to prevent another direct assault, a fort on a low hill on the coastal plain became the headquarters, and gun batteries were installed on the higher ground overlooking the sea. The expected attack duly arrived when, on 26 September 1842, a fleet of 29 British ships

---

[1] Harry G. Gelber, *Opium, Soldiers and Evangelicals: England's 1840-42 war with China, and its aftermath* (London: Palgrave, 2004), p. 109.

[2] Gelber, *Opium, Soldiers and Evangelicals,* pp. 117-8.

[3] Zhejiang-shen Zhoushan-Shi Zhenxie Wenshi hi Xiexi Weiyuunhui (eds.), *Yapian Zhansheng Zai Zhoushan* [Opium War in Zhoushan] (Beijing: Zhongguo Wenshi Chubanshe, 2005), p. 333.

sailed into Dinghai Bay. A British commentator observed that "every hill on coast in the vicinity of Dinghai was crowned with a battery of apparent strength".[4] On 1 October soldiers of the Westmoreland Regiment (the 55th) landed at the foot of the higher ground to the west. After capturing these heights they were able to bypass the coastal defences, march inland and take control of Dinghai. Their task was made easier by the fact that the slopes of a hill in the northwest corner of the city led straight down into the streets, removing the need to scale its walls. The Royal Irish Rifles, meanwhile, attacked the sea defences and stormed the headquarters.[5]

A few days later a British force left its new base at Zhoushan and launched an assault on the mainland. It soon overcame the defences guarding the Yong Estuary at Zhenhai and sailed downriver to capture the populous city of Ningbo. After wintering there the British then moved north, advanced down the Yangtze River and blockaded the entrance to the Grand Canal. As the gateway to the main commercial artery between the Yangtze Valley and Beijing, this forced the Chinese authorities to negotiate terms. The result was the Treaty of Nanjing signed on 29 August 1842, the first of the "Unequal Treaties", under which Hong Kong was officially ceded to the British and five ports – Canton, Xiamen (Amoy), Ningbo, Fuzhou and Shanghai – were opened for trade.

The Westmoreland Regiment and China

After the assault on Dinghai in October 1841, the Westmoreland Regiment remained on Zhoushan Island until 1844. It was then garrisoned for four years in nearby Ningbo, but this was to be its last round of service in China, as its next assignment would be much closer to home in Ulster. Today the Westmoreland Regiment no longer exists as such, for it was amalgamated in the 1880s with other units in the region to form the King's Own

---

[4] Rev. Wright in *Allom's China* (1844), cited in Keith Stevens and Jennifer Welch, "Monument to the Westmoreland Regiment the 55th Regiment of Foot in Dinghai City on Zhoushan Island", in *Journal of the Hong Kong Branch of the Asiatic Society*, vol.3, p. 385.
[5] Gelber, *Opium, Soldiers and Evangelicals,* p. 128.

Border Regiment. The regiment's legacy, though, is still remembered in its home county of Westmoreland (now Cumbria) in the northwest of England close to the border with Scotland, an area renowned for the scenic beauty of the Lake District National Park.

This picturesque corner of England may seem an unlikely place to find mementoes of battles fought in China, but examples can be seen at the King's Own Royal Border Regimental Museum in Carlisle Castle, which traces the regiment's history from its formation in 1702. Two maps brought back to England after the Opium War are now kept here. One is a British chart of Zhenjiang, the town on the Yangtze River where the fleet blockaded the entrance to the Grand Canal. The other is a Chinese sketch portraying the defences around Dinghai, including the walls along the seafront and the headquarters on the low hill which the British called the "joss house". A war trophy can also be found inside the local parish church in Kendal, situated in the heart of the Lake District. Hanging on a wall next to the regimental memorial is a Chinese imperial standard captured during the assault on "Chusan Heights".[6]

Such military symbols can be used to evoke a complex mixture of loyalty and pride. In the case of the British Army they consciously recall the exploits of those who fought for the "colours" in the past in order to focus soldiers' minds on current operations. For example, the King"s Own Royal Border Regimental Colours and Battle Honours contain a wealth of information embroidered in text and images. The honours cite battles in which the Westmoreland Regiment took part, such as "Peninsula", "Corunna" and "Waterloo" during the Napoleonic Wars. Also featured are "Sevastopol" *[sic]* from the Crimean War, "Abyssinia" *[sic]* and "Afganistan" *[sic]*. Images portrayed in the Colours include the red rose of Lancaster and four lions. "Chusan" does not appear as such, but embroidered prominently in gold at the bottom of the standard is a distinctly oriental dragon in rampant profile bearing a banner emblazoned with the word "China".[7]

---

[6] P. Bruce, "An Imperial Chinese Banner Preserved in Kendal, England", in *Journal HK Br RAS* 23 (1983), pp. 202-3.

[7] King's Own Border Regiment Website (**http://www.army.mod.uk/**

Recently, the Border regiment, too, disappeared as an independent unit as the result of some major structural reforms in the British Army. To commemorate the event, the regiment embarked on a project called "Exercise Global Dragon", clearly a reference to the dragon embroidered on the Colours. This was how it was described on the regimental website:

In July 2006, The Kings Own Royal Border Regiment will pass into history when the Regiment merges with the other Infantry Regiments from the North West of England, The King's Regiment and The Queen's Lancashire Regiment, to form the Duke of Lancaster's Regiment. This exercise [Global Dragon] is all about the legacy of one the oldest Regiments of the British Army. The Regiment intends to mount journeys on 4 continents as far afield as Cuba, South Africa, Ethiopia, the Ukraine, Turkey, Iraq, Pakistan, India and China as well as the better known battlefield sites of the 1st and 2nd World Wars. The journey to the 59 locations will all happen over the same week in June 2006, involving 192 men using all forms of transport from airliner to train, car to mule to reach some of the more inaccessible areas of the world. The event will focus on the human angle – not a triumphant record of past military engagements but a more reflective journey by the young men of today's Army to see and experience at first hand the realities of what their forbears undertook. The event will also be a major organisational and technical challenge.[8]

Revisiting the Battle of "Chusan Heights"

As part of Global Dragon, four soldiers from the Royal Border Regiment visited Dinghai on Wednesday 14 June 2006. It was a mission in marked contrast to their previous assignment as they had just recently returned from active service in Iraq. As the leader

---

korbr/history/battle_honours.htm). See also Stuart Eastwood, *A Pictorial History of the King's Own Regiment (Lancaster) 1680-1980* (Kettering: Silver Link Publishing Ltd, 1991), pp. 183-5.

[8] King's Own Border Regiment Website (**http://www.army.mod.uk/ korbr/index.htm**).

of the party explained at the time, "the main point of the visit will be to conduct a Service of Remembrance at a relevant location yet to be established, ideally a memorial if it still exists".[9] The journey placed their regimental memory of the Battle of Chusan Heights in immediate juxtaposition with local recollections and perspectives on the conflict present in Zhoushan today.

This battle clearly holds some meaning for serving personnel in one regiment of the British Army, but it is not a name familiar to many people in contemporary British society. Chusan Heights does not feature among the battles which, for varying reasons, live on in popular memory, from Waterloo and Sebastopol to Balaclava and Khartoum. During the nineteenth century it perhaps held more resonance for the Victorian public, notwithstanding the ambivalence surrounding the wars with China even then. Three P&O ships, for example, have been named "Chusan". The first, built in 1850, tragically sank, but a second was built in 1884; the third, built in 1950, was a sister ship of the famous SS *Oriana*. Taken out of service in the 1980s she was later converted into a floating theme park in the city of Dalian in northern China until being finally overhauled in 2005.

On Zhoushan Island itself, the day the British came back to attack Dinghai in 1841 has long since become an integral part of the local heritage. More broadly, it is familiar also to high school students throughout China as one of the key sites where concerted resistance was organised against the foreign invaders during the "First Opium War". The opening section of Chapter One in high school textbooks on the modern history of China is devoted to this short campaign.[10] The theme represents a clear break with the traditional history that went before, and marks the opening salvo of the "Western intrusion", heralding a period conceived as a time of continuous struggle which continues to inform Chinese historical perspectives today. On page five is a "list of eight patriotic generals" who led the resistance against the British, three

---

[9] Captain Robert Small, 6 June 2006, the University of Nottingham Ningbo, China; the author of this paper acted as the party's guide on their visit to Zhoushan.
[10] Renmin Jiaoyu Chebanshe Rishi-Shi (eds.), *Zhongguo Jindai Xiandai Shi* [Chinese Modern and Contemporary History] (Beijing; Renmin Jiaoyu Chunbanshe, 2002), vol. 1, pp. 1-6.

of whom died at the Battle of Zhoushan.[11] In this Chinese representation of the event it is these men – Ge Yunfei, Zheng Guohong and Wang Xipeng – who are the central actors. On the battlefield of Chusan Heights itself, it is predominantly their story which is commemorated and retold in prose and verse.[12]

Access to Zhoushan Island today is by a forty-minute ferry ride from the mainland, and from the terminal the city of Dinghai is then a short drive away along the coast. No longer confined to the walls the British knew in the 1840s, buildings now sprawl across the coastal plain. In the wake of recent economic development it has become a modern city with a population of 500,000, and further expansion is anticipated once a new bridge now under construction joins Zhoushan with the mainland in 2008.

The higher ground to the west is easily recognisable as the place where the Westmoreland Regiment carried out the assault on Chusan Heights. The entire site is now occupied by the "Zhoushan Opium War Memorial Park". There has long since been a park of some description here, but as the plaques at the entrance describe, this underwent a major renovation during the mid-1990s before a grand reopening ceremony on 20 June 1997 attended by a crowd of over 1,000 people.[13] It is no coincidence that this was also the year in which sovereignty over Hong Kong was handed back to China.[14]

In 1996, while renovation was still underway, the park in Zhoushan was named as a "centre of patriotic education" at provincial level, and in 2001 it received recognition at national level as well.[15] Together with other parks and museums constructed at the time, it can be seen as a symbolic and highly

[11] Renmin Jiaoyu Chebanshe Rishi-Shi (eds.), *Zhongguo Jindai Xiandai Shi*, p. 5

[12] See, for example, "The Death of Ge Yunfei" in Zhejiang-shen Zhoushan-Shi Zhenxie Wenshi hi Xiexi Weiyuunhui (eds.), *Yapian Zhansheng Zai Zhoushan,* pp. 299-300.

[13] Zhejiang-shen Zhoushan-Shi Zhenxie Wenshi hi Xiexi Weiyuunhui (eds.), *Yapian Zhansheng Zai Zhoushan,* p. 324.

[14] Zhejiang-shen Zhoushan-Shi Zhenxie Wenshi hi Xiexi Weiyuunhui (eds.), *Yapian Zhansheng Zai Zhoushan,* p. 333.

[15] Zhejiang-shen Zhoushan-Shi Zhenxie Wenshi hi Xiexi Weiyuunhui (eds.), *Yapian Zhansheng Zai Zhoushan,* p. 335.

visible extension of the literature of national humiliation (*guochi*), which became so prevalent in the 1990s. Consciously promoted by patriotic educators, this has placed a new emphasis on "the Chinese people's defiant struggle" during "the imperialist interval in Chinese history".[16] The campaign is targeted mainly at a younger generation that has no first-hand memory of the pain and suffering experienced by their forbears. During the first seven years after the park reopened more than 300,000 visitors were recorded, with special attention given to educating "junior high and elementary schoolchildren".[17]

Today the park is thickly wooded, unlike the scene in a British watercolour sketch painted at the time of the battle, which perhaps used artistic licence to portray a file of redcoats marching up a bare ridge.[18] Near the entrance some memorials in polished granite bear messages in praise of the defending garrison's patriotic valour. Among the trees higher up the slopes are a few older, weathered graves of Chinese soldiers, who died defending the heights. In a clearing on the site of the first height there is a monument in memory of Zhen Guohong, the first of the three generals killed during the assault. The imperial standard now hanging in Kendal Church was probably taken from this spot.

Further inland is the second height, which was under the command of Wang Xipeng. This is the highest point in the park, and here, overlooking the city of Dinghai is a towering monument of three pillars, one for each general. At the base a group of larger-than-life stone busts represents the generals with stern expressions facing the bay, and behind a relief portrays them as immovable giants driving the invader into the sea. All accounts agree, in fact, that at one stage some British troops advancing along the coastal walls were forced back by Commander-in-Chief Ge Yunfei. Further inland, on the next height along the ridge, is an older building dating to 1854, which also contains life-size statues of the

---

[16] Paul A. Cohen, *China Unbound; evolving perspectives on the Chinese past* (London: Routledge-Curzon, 2003), pp. 148, 167.
[17] Zhejiang-shen Zhoushan-Shi Zhenxie Wenshi hi Xiexi Weiyuunhui (eds.), *Yapian Zhansheng Zai Zhoushan,* p. 276
[18] Zhejiang-shen Zhoushan-Shi Zhenxie Wenshi hi Xiexi Weiyuunhui (eds.), *Yapian Zhansheng Zai Zhoushan,* cover illustration

three generals.[19] Immediately below this is the Zhoushan Opium War Memorial Museum, which was fitted out to coincide with the grand opening of the park in June 1997.[20]

For the most part the narrative recounted for visitors to the museum corresponds with the story known to soldiers of the Royal Border Regiment. All agree, for example, that the walls built along the seafront forced the Westmoreland Regiment to concentrate its attack on scaling the ridge of "Chusan Heights" to the west. Some details, however, do not feature in British accounts. For example, on the day of the assault the bay was shrouded in mist, making it difficult for the defending garrison to see the invaders' movements.[21] Also, the British launched no less than nine attacks and managed to take the ridge only after local informers showed them a path up the slope. This appears to be consistent with a Chinese account which claims that "the British suffered heavy casualties", whereas the British record holds that the Westmoreland Regiment captured the heights with the loss of just two men.[22]

Interwoven into the Chinese narrative can perhaps be discerned a stylised subtext in which key elements – treachery and the weather – contributed to thwarting the three generals' heroic defence of Dinghai. Not only does this cast a tragic note on the episode but conveys a message on the importance of unity, a theme familiar to Chinese television audiences from dramas which re-enact the exploits of "civilian soldiers" (*minbin*) during the 1930s and 1940s. Such links reinforce the impression that contemporary Chinese representations of the Battle of Zhoushan can only be fully understood in the context of a wider victimhood discourse on resistance to outside attack in the modern era.

On a related note, Chinese accounts have often pointed to what has been perceived as the overwhelming numerical superiority of

[19] Zhejiang-shen Zhoushan-Shi Zhenxie Wenshi hi Xiexi Weiyuunhui (eds.), *Yapian Zhansheng Zai Zhoushan,* p. 335.

[20] Zhejiang-shen Zhoushan-Shi Zhenxie Wenshi hi Xiexi Weiyuunhui (eds.), *Yapian Zhansheng Zai Zhoushan,* p. 329.

[21] Zhejiang-shen Zhoushan-Shi Zhenxie Wenshi hi Xiexi Weiyuunhui (eds.), *Yapian Zhansheng Zai Zhoushan,* p. 294.

[22] Tung Chi-Ming, *An Outline History of China* (Beijing: Foreign Languages Press, 1959), p. 215. Gelber, *Opium, Soldiers and Evangelicals,* p. 128.

the British troops, a point of detail which may have been used to help subsequent generations come to terms with the result. The British victory, however, was probably due more to a combination of technological superiority and the discipline of seasoned troops. Traditional estimates of the invading force have been in the region of 30,000 and research as late as the 1980s referred to a British force of "not less than 20,000 men".[23] Only recently have conscious efforts been made to present a more detached perspective, with estimates of the British numbers now reduced to no more than 3,000.[24] As such, Chinese scholarship has begun to converge with English records which place the invasion force in the region of 2,700 men.[25]

Finally, on their visit to Dinghai in June 2006 the four British soldiers succeeded in locating the memorial they were looking for on the slopes of the hill their forbears called the "joss house". Today the site of a radio tower, the top of the hill is still girdled by the walls of the old fort and one-time headquarters of Commander-in-Chief Ge Yunfei. On the northern slope just below these walls is a stone memorial built by the regiment in classical style, although the inscription it once bore has clearly been erased at some later undetermined date. The message has not been lost, however, as a British visitor to the island in the 1880s recorded the inscription as follows: "Sacred to The Memory of 11 Sergeants, 13 Corporals, 4 Drummers and 403 Privates Of H.M. 55th Regt, who were killed in action or died from disease while serving in China from the 14th July 1841 to the 22nd February 1844."[26] Also recorded were the thirty or so gravestones inscribed with the names of those, most of them victims of disease, who died during the British occupation of the island, among them ten

---

[23] Cheng Minde, "Yapian Zhansheng Zhong Dinghai zhi Zhang de Yingjun Bingri Wenti Chutan" [Preliminary Investigation on the Question of the Strength of the British Forces at Dinghai in the Opium War] in Zhejiang-shen Zhoushan-Shi Zhenxie Wenshi hi Xiexi Weiyuunhui (eds.), *Yapian Zhansheng Zai Zhoushan*, p. 207.

[24] Cheng, in Zhejiang-shen Zhoushan-Shi Zhenxie Wenshi hi Xiexi Weiyuunhui (eds.), *Yapian Zhansheng Zai Zhoushan*, p. 214.

[25] Gelber, *Opium, Soldiers and Evangelicals*, p. 128.

[26] Stevens and Welch, "Monument to the Westmoreland Regiment" pp. 386-7.

officers' wives and two infants.[27]

Close to this monument are two other more recent memorials of Chinese origin built in memory of the British who died in Zhoushan. One bears an inscription in unsimplified script, which would appear to date to the 1920s.[28] The other is relatively new, a gesture of local pride put up in 2002 to commemorate the establishment of the new Zhoushan Municipal Government. These illustrate how memories of the Westmoreland Regiment and those who died in its cause have, to some extent now been incorporated in the fabric of local heritage in Zhoushan.

Today, the storming of Chusan Heights and the resistance organised in Dinghai are recalled through competing textual narratives, fractured images and such memorials commemorating the fallen. While recollections in Britain may be prompted by occasional army reforms and the amalgamation of a regiment now serving in the Middle East, in Zhoushan a newly renovated park contributes to ongoing efforts in China to remind the younger generation of their forbears' patriotic spirit. In terms of the scale of audience they address these narratives hardly bear comparison, but there are unmistakable similarities in representation. Courage and duty are symbolically invoked for brave generals and regimental colours alike. Where the narratives seem to diverge is mostly in response to motives imposed by and for later generations, including subsequent memories superimposed and often far removed from the experience of those who fought on Chusan Heights in October 1841.

[27] Stevens and Welch, "Monument to the Westmoreland Regiment" pp. 389-91.
[28] Stevens and Welch, "Monument to the Westmoreland Regiment" p. 391.

CINEMA AT THE BORDER

Panaméricas Utópicas: Entranced and Transient Nations in *I Am Cuba* and *Land in Trance*[1]

Lúcia Nagib
University of Leeds

In this chapter I look at two political films, *Land in Trance* (Glauber Rocha, 1967) and *I Am Cuba* (Mikhail Kalatozov, 1964), which address the subject of the nation through the enactment of trance. Rejecting all forms of naturalistic account, both films adopt a series of anti-realist devices, such as poetic language, synecdoche, personification, parable and allegory, as a means of expanding the concept of the nation beyond territorial borders and conveying the meaning of revolution through the film form rather than its content.

Let us begin by looking at the original title of Glauber Rocha's film, *Terra em transe,* which has been translated into English both as *Land in Anguish* and *Land in Trance.* I will give preference to the latter, as it preserves the word "trance", crucial to this analysis. *Terra* (land) is another important word, as it connects three Rocha films which became known as the *trilogia da terra,* or "land trilogy", of which *Land in Trance* is the second part. They include *Deus e o diabo na terra do sol* (1964), translated as *Black God, White Devil,* but actually meaning *God and the Devil in the Land of the Sun,* and *A idade da terra* (1980), or *The Age of the Earth.*

Like the English word "land", *terra* means both any given territory and the home country (that is, the motherland or the nation). But unlike its English equivalent, *terra* also means the planet Earth. In Glauber's trilogy, the term *terra* circulates through all these meanings. In *Black God, White Devil,* the "land of the sun" refers to the Brazilian dry backlands, a territory of poverty known as *sertão,* which functions as a synecdoche for the entire Brazilian nation. In *Land in Trance,* the land is expanded to encompass all Latin American countries which, according to Glauber's vision, shared the same historical determination. In *The Age of the Earth,* the term *terra* refers to a land whose political processes acquire global resonance.

<hr>

[1] A shorter, earlier version of this essay was published in *Hispanic Research Journal* 8, 1 (February 2007), pp. 79-90.

My second object of study is the film *Soy Cuba (I Am Cuba)*, released in the same year 1964, when the first part of Rocha's "land trilogy", *Black God, White Devil,* was launched. In *I Am Cuba,* national identity is expressed in the very title, which contains the name of a real country. But the title also makes us aware of a synecdochic stance, that is, a part which speaks for the whole, for it is a human voice in the first person that claims to be the land itself.

Just as important as the concept of nation and territory in these films is that of "trance" and its relations with transit, transformation and revolution. *Transe,* in Portuguese, is an overarching word, which includes ideas of "distress", "risk", "danger", "hazard", "crisis" and "anxiety". It suggests "struggle", "fight", the state of a medium possessed by a spirit as well as "passage" and "death". In English, the word "trance" has the more restricted meaning of a sleep-like state, caused, for example, by hypnosis, in which one concentrates on one's thoughts remaining oblivious of the world around. For the purposes of this analysis, I will be using the word "trance" in the broader sense of the Portuguese term.

In both *Land in Trance* and *I Am Cuba,* trance is a structural feature. Not only do they focus on characters in a permanent state of mental upheaval, in countries going through revolutionary processes, but ideas of trance and revolution are conveyed by the film form itself. The similarities between these films are indeed so striking, that one would naturally assume that Rocha had seen *I Am Cuba* before conceiving of *Land in Trance.* However, my investigation of this hypothesis has produced no conclusive results. Apparently, Rocha never had the chance to visit Cuba before 1971, when he finally went there as an exile for a prolonged sojourn. Some sources consulted have suggested that he might have seen *I Am Cuba* in one of the film festivals he attended during his tours through the United States, Mexico and Europe, in 1964-65. However, the film travelled little upon its launch and was prohibited in the US at that time. Furthermore, Rocha was a prolific writer and used to comment in writing on all his cinematic and cultural experiences, but no mention of *I Am Cuba* is to be found in any of his collected letters, articles, interviews and manifestoes. The only suggestion that he was familiar with Mikhail

Kalatozov's work is a review of his *The Cranes Are Flying* (1957) he published in 1960, four years before *I Am Cuba* was released.[2]

The fact remains that Rocha had nurtured a bottomless admiration for Cuba, Fidel Castro and Che Guevara from the time of the Cuban revolution, in 1959. Since the early 1960s he had been working on a film script with the Spanish title of *América nuestra,* inspired by the Cuban revolution. From 1960 onwards, Rocha was in regular contact with Alfredo Guevara, the president of the Instituto Cubano del Arte e Industria Cinematográfica (ICAIC), who for several years made all possible efforts to overcome diplomatic obstacles and bring Rocha to Cuba to shoot *America Nuestra,* all to no avail. Che Guevara's death in 1967 put an end to the project, though parts of the 1966 script of *América Nuestra* were used in *Land in Trance*.

Until further evidence is produced, I can only see the haunting coincidences between *I Am Cuba* and *Land in Trance* as some sort of "trance", or spiritual transit between filmmakers interested in interpreting social revolution through revolutionary filmmaking. The channel through which they communicated over national borders was certainly their passion for the film medium, a cinephilia which, since the French *nouvelle vague* and its *politique des auteurs,* had been suffusing the international circulation of images through cinematic homage and citation. Rocha's own *auteur* pantheon included Godard, Welles and Buñuel, whose influences are easily detectable in *Land in Trance*. In *I Am Cuba,* Expressionist and other German influences, particularly from Fritz Lang, are noticeable, as well as from Marcel Camus and the portrait of a foreign country he produced in *Black Orpheus* (1959). Above all, neither of the two films could be conceived without the experience of Eisenstein, his vertical montage and anti-realist concept of revolutionary cinema.

[2] Glauber Rocha, "*Quando voam as cegonhas*", in *Diário de Notícias* (Salvador: 12 June 1960). A mention of this article, which remains unpublished in Rocha's collected writings, is found in *Glauber Rocha – Scritti sul cinema* (Venice: XLIII Mostra Internazionale del Cinema, 1986), p. 219.

The global land

Land in Trance and *I Am Cuba* prove to be siblings from their opening images. Both go back to the early history of the Americas to explain the current political situation. Both resort to the discovery mythology to globalise the history of a single country.[3]

Land in Trance is introduced by a long and slow aerial sequence-shot of the sea occupying the totality of the frame. The music in the background is *candomblé*[4] drumming and singing, whose function is to induce mystic trance. The camera that slides from left to right captures the sea's rounded surface as if it were the globe itself illuminated by the sun's metallic glow. Credits are superimposed on the images, while the camera glides over mountains covered with dense forest, followed by a valley through which a river winds its way. There are no signs of human presence in this pristine scenery, over which appears the title in parentheses: (Eldorado, inner country, Atlantic).

I Am Cuba also begins with long, smooth aerial shots of the sea, leading to the Caribbean island's immaculate hills and palm tree forests. In the black and white photography the sea presents a metallic glow, while the palm trees acquire a white shine under the sun.[5] The camera eventually stops before a white wooden cross at the sea shore, bearing an inscription which marks Christopher Columbus's visit to the island. "Cuba's" female voice-over then recites the poem "Soy Cuba", which makes up the voice-over commentary throughout the film:

> Once, Christopher Columbus landed here. He wrote in his diary: "This is the most beautiful land ever seen by human

[3] For a detailed analysis of sea imagery in Brazilian and other films, see Chapter 1 in Lúcia Nagib, *Brazil on Screen – Cinema Novo, New Cinema, Utopia* (London, New York: I.B. Tauris, 2007).

[4] Afro-Brazilian religion, of Yoruba origin, which worships deities called *orixás* (orishas).

[5] This effect was achieved with the use of negative stock sensitive to infrared rays, provided by the Russian army, according to information contained in the documentary film *Soy Cuba – the Siberian Mammoth* (*Soy Cuba – o mamute siberiano*), directed by the Brazilian director Vicente Ferraz, in 2005.

eyes". Thank you, Señor Columbus. When you saw me for the first time, I was singing and laughing. I waved the fronds of my palms to greet your sails. I thought your ships brought happiness.

In both cases, paradise regained is only presented to be immediately denied. In *Land in Trance* the solemn arrival in Eldorado is abruptly interrupted by the insertion of various sequences of action and violence that retell the coup led by Porfírio Díaz and his triumphal arrival at the deserted beach. In *I Am Cuba*, the film goes on to show, under the palm trees, the shacks and the miserable conditions in which Cubans live nowadays.

We are actually looking at a re-elaboration of the sea metaphor as employed in films such as *The Battleship Potemkin* (1925), by Eisenstein, in which images of an agitated sea suggest revolution. Rocha had used a similar metaphor in the final scenes of *Black God, White Devil*, when, in a revolutionary, apocalyptical reversal, the backlands are replaced by a sea in turmoil. In *Land in Trance*, however, the placid, maritime prelude, representing the European discoverers' utopia, is immediately denied by the story of a land in political chaos and a population in trance.

In Rocha's film, history and geography are compressed in an allegorical country, which is a patchwork of allusions to several Latin American historical episodes. The basic storyline is a loose interpretation of recent events in Brazil, which led to the installation of a military dictatorship. In the film, the failure of revolution is attributed to the left wing's alliance with a populist politician, who proves unable to resist the pressure of international capital and the ascension of a despotic leader. The rendering of these facts is done through the merging of contemporary Brazilian characters with the first European discoverers, religious leaders and native inhabitants of the Americas, as well as political figures of various provenances. The present-day country fuses with the myth and becomes Eldorado, its main province is named after the Portuguese province of Alecrim and its president is called Porfírio Díaz, like the famous Mexican dictator. Among them, the protagonist, Paulo Martins, wanders in permanent trance, torn as he is between different social classes and interests.

Also in *I Am Cuba,* the maritime overture is used as a means to deconstruct the discovery mythology. The film's multilayered structure juxtaposes the stories of four different characters, a prostitute, a student, a peasant and a guerrilla, who experience in different ways the nefarious consequences of colonial domination and sugar cane exploitation, in place in the island since its discovery by the Europeans. As in *Land in Trance,* the characters' rebellion against oppression finds expression through trance. Although drawing on the real story of the Cuban revolution, all characters are outspokenly fictional and their origin is to be found in cinematic cross-referencing and myth, rather than history.

Trance and national crisis in *Land in Trance*

In Glauber Rocha's films, ambiguous, contradictory characters permanently torn between the opposing forces of God and the Devil, or between the perks of the upper classes and the desperate needs of the oppressed, fall into a trance that lends their crisis a metaphysical dimension. The trance of the protagonists, as well as that of the masses, resonates through all technical aspects of his films, including music, sound and camera work. Ivana Bentes goes as far as identifying the process of trance as "the first figuration of Glauber's thought and cinema".

> "Trance" means transition, passage, possession, the process of becoming. In order to fall into a crisis or trance, one needs to be penetrated or possessed by the other. Glauber turned "trance" into a form of experimentation and experience. [For him] to fall into a trance is to be in phase with an object or situation, to experience it from inside.[6]

In *Land in Trance,* Ismail Xavier sees Rocha's use of what he calls "the *transe* metaphor" as a way of characterising the national crisis.[7] Indeed, Brazil's 1964 military coup, as recounted in the film,

---

[6] Ivana Bentes, "Introdução", in Glauber Rocha, *Cartas ao mundo,* ed. Ivana Bentes (São Paulo: Companhia das Letras, 1997), p. 26.
[7] Ismail Xavier, *Allegories of Underdevelopment: Aesthetics and Politics in Modern Brazilian Cinema* (Minneapolis, London: University of Minnesota Press, 1997), p. 82.

puts an end not only to the revolutionary hopes of the left, but also to the national project which had inspired Cinema Novo's first phase, including Rocha's ground-breaking *Black God, White Devil*. The defence of the national, in early Cinema Novo, included the representation of Brazil through its impoverished, rural backlands in the Northeast, the *sertão,* whose images were held responsible for the "national" quality of Brazilian cinema's photography. As remarked by Galvão and Bernardet, in the 1960s,

> ... the photography of the northeast [had become] Brazilian cinema's "trade mark". It was valued not only for its adequacy to the reality conveyed, but also because it opposed a photographic style considered foreign.[8]

Land in Trance marks Rocha's departure from the "land of the sun", which disappears together with the filmmaker's faith in the nation. As a consequence, the search for realism is replaced by anti-realism. It is true that *Black God, White Devil* contained a number of anti-naturalistic devices, such as theatrical acting, discontinuous editing and a noisy, polyphonic soundtrack echoing the religious trance of the masses. But there was an effort to characterise Brazil as a real country, through precise historical references, such as the rebellion of Canudos, identifiable locations, such as the northeastern *sertão,* and true historical characters, such as the *cangaceiros* (the *sertão*'s outlaws). It is the demise of the national project in Brazil's real history that enables Rocha to break away from such realist constraints and fully develop his Latin American project. As he himself declared at that time,

> [...] the awareness that Brazil, Mexico, Argentina, Peru, Bolivia, etc. are part of the same block of North-American exploitation and that exploitation is one of the most profound causes of underdevelopment is becoming increasingly consistent and, more importantly, popular. The notion of Latin America overrides the notion of nationalisms.[9]

---

[8] Maria Rita Galvão and Jean-Claude Bernardet, *O nacional e o popular na cultura brasileira: cinema* (São Paulo: Braziliense/Embrafilme, 1983), p. 204.
[9] Glauber Rocha, "Teoria e prática do cinema latino-americano 67", in *Revolução do Cinema Novo* (São Paulo: CosacNaify, 2004), p. 83.

In order to turn this vision into film, he created a vacuum of realism within his stylistic sources. As noted by Xavier, *Land in Trance* draws on the artistic movements which came before and after realism, that is to say, the medieval or baroque allegory, on the one hand, and modernism and the avant-gardes, on the other.[10]

The film is constructed with the help of synecdochic procedures, through which a subjective point of view is totalised to account for the state of a land as a whole. This land, in its turn, is at the same time transnational, transcontinental and mythical. The story is narrated in flashback by the poet and journalist Paulo Martins, who stumbles in agony on sand dunes after being shot by the police. His feverish and fragmentary recollection of his relations with the dictator Porfírio Díaz and the populist leader Felipe Vieira are recounted through discontinuous editing and a hysterical, asynchronous soundtrack, often overlapping the sounds of operas (especially Carlos Gomes and Verdi), machinegun shots and screams. Devoted to sculpting reality, rather than capturing it, the unsteady, hand-held camera becomes the perfect tool for the creation of trance.

Rocha coined the word *parabolizar*, or "turn into a parable", to describe the narrative structure of *Land in Trance*. As Eduardo Escorel, the film editor, recalls, the director's intention was to change "all linear narrative into parabolic". Escorel unearths from the Greek root of the word "parable" the very definition of Rocha's cinema: the idea of "shooting to the side" or "splintering".[11] The subjective point of view, in *Land in Trance,* is the way through which the "splintering" effect is achieved. All dialogues are contaminated by the protagonist Paulo's metaphysical preoccupations and poetic thinking, a language which combines Mário Faustino's tragic poems with others authored by Rocha himself. The outside world is thus denied an objective representation, as it is distorted in accordance with Paulo's permanent state of trance.

As Ismail Xavier points out, allegory and condensation of

[10] Ismail Xavier, "Prefácio", in Rocha, *Revolução do Cinema Novo,* p. 24.
[11] Eduardo Escorel, "Glauber Rocha: a estrela parabólica", in *Adivinhadores de água* (São Paulo: CosacNaify, 2005), p. 78.

history, in *Land in Trance,* are used to create ambiguity and enigma, rather than enlightenment.[12] The same is true for its subjective narrative, which Xavier compares to Pasolini's theory of "the free indirect subjective" as defined in his essay on "Cinema of Poetry":

> [...] in *Land in Trance,* whether a scene is explicitly subject to the poet's interior monologue or not, the entire narration is contaminated by the poet's state of mind. [...] The "disturbed mind" is not only the character's but also that of the invisible narrator.[13]

Xavier finds similarities between this technique and what Eisenstein termed "interior monologue", a discourse which combines "the feverish race of thoughts" with "outer reality".[14]

Interior monologues are indeed a prevailing feature in *Land in Trance,* in which conversations easily turn into declamation, citation and recitation. Robert Stam refers to the film as "a veritable essay on the intersection of art and politics" in which people "find it normal to address each other in poetry".[15] In Rocha's own view, "the Latin American political avant-gardes [are] led by intellectuals, and therefore poetry precedes the gun".[16]

In his effort to blur the boundaries between Latin American countries, Rocha, in *Land in Trance,* installed the leaders of Eldorado in palaces in the middle of an unidentifiable jungle, where they debate their strategies in poetic language and operatic demeanours, constantly resorting to Spanish terms. Moving away from the desperate masses on the arid backlands to focus on the powerful installed on the top of lush mountains, the camera ends

---

[12] Xavier, *Allegories of Underdevelopment: Aesthetics and Politics in Modern Brazilian Cinema,* p. 20.

[13] Xavier, *Allegories of Underdevelopment: Aesthetics and Politics in Modern Brazilian Cinema,* pp. 66ff.

[14] Xavier, *Allegories of Underdevelopment: Aesthetics and Politics in Modern Brazilian Cinema,* pp. 62ff.

[15] Robert Stam, "Land in Anguish", in Robert Stam and Randal Johnson (eds.), *Brazilian Cinema* (expanded edition; New York: Columbia UP, 1982), pp. 149, 156.

[16] Glauber Rocha, "Tricontinental 67", in *A Revolução do Cinema Novo,* p. 107.

up conveying a foreign, uncanny view of the country, which, in some mysterious way, is surprisingly similar to the portrayal of Cuba through Russian eyes in *I Am Cuba.*

I Am Cuba and the foreign land

Although frequently, and wrongly, associated with Soviet social realism, *I Am Cuba* also relies entirely on anti-realist techniques. It was photographed by the extraordinary cameraman Sergei Urusevsky, who in this film created the most spectacular sequence-shots ever seen on screen, on the basis of a script written by the Russian poet Yevgeni Yevtushenko and the Cuban writer Enrique Pineda Barnet.

The film is, thus, mainly the vision of foreigners, according to testimonies of members of the crew themselves. "As far as Cuba is concerned, we didn't know about their culture or their tongue, we only knew its location on the map", says, for example, Sacha Calzatti, the camera operator in *I Am Cuba,* in an interview included in the Brazilian documentary *Soy Cuba – The Siberian Mammoth* (2005), by Vicente Ferraz. As documented in Ferraz's film, the country in *I Am Cuba* was never recognised as their own by Cuban audiences or even by those Cubans who were involved in its making. It was a complete flop on its release in Havana and was shelved after just a week's screening in the cinemas.

A foreign vision of Cuba is indeed perceptible in all aspects of the film. Havana is photographed in such a way as to give prominence to its modern socialist architecture. Huge buildings in vast spaces lend it the looks of a soviet city. The film's cityscapes are actually reminiscent of those in *The Cranes Are Flying,* the Cannes Golden Palm-winning film directed and photographed by the same duo, Kalatozov-Urusevsky.

Images drawn from various cinemas of the world were used to cover the gaps in local knowledge. The characterisation of the actress, Luz Maria Collazo, who plays the virgin/prostitute Maria/Betty, turned her into a kind of clone of Marpesa Dawn in *Black Orpheus,* a film with curious links with Brazil, whose pioneering, and highly influential, quality resides precisely in conveying the idea of a "tropical country" (Brazil) and a "tropical people" (the Brazilians) to foreign audiences.

In *I Am Cuba,* the citation is made through a critical view. In Camus's film the *favela* is an idyllic place, with a happy people permanently dancing and singing samba. Eurydice is the black virgin who lives in an "interesting" *favela*, and trance, of course, is a prominent feature, through which the Greek Orphic myths acquire Afro-Brazilian overtones. This was certainly not overlooked by Kalatozov, who made sure to introduce African wooden idols in the nightclub scene in which Betty falls into a trance, in *I Am Cuba.* However, in this film, poverty is denied all touristy interest when Betty says, about the slum where she lives: "No, senõr, no es interesante", and then proceeds to show her miserable quarters to her lustful American client.

Another feature which accounts for the unfortunate career of *I Am Cuba* in Cuba is its operatic timing, which prompted some of its Cuban collaborators to reject it as contrary to Cuba's real life tempo.[17] As much as *Land in Trance,* whose unreal operatic construction caused an initial uproar before the film was hailed as a master piece, *I Am Cuba* was clearly not conceived to produce cathartic illusionism, but rather to allow the viewer to penetrate, understand and appreciate the meanders and subtleties of cinematic techniques, which the filmmakers believed could be equally or more revolutionary than objective history.

Personification and the myth

Both *Land in Trance* and *I Am Cuba* rely on types representing their classes, rather than on detail. In the former, there are: the poet/journalist Paulo Martins; the poor peasant; the trade union leader; the priest; the father figure, Porfírio Díaz; the mother figure, Sara; the mute Silvia, who incarnates the prostituted, objectified woman; the company Explint, representing international capital; and Julio Fuentes, the media tycoon. In *I Am Cuba,* we have the student; the revolutionary leader; the double figure of Maria/Betty; the poor peasant; the rich Americans; and the company United Fruit, representing international capital.

---

[17] See interviews in *Soy Cuba – o mamute siberiano,* documentary film by Vicente Ferraz.

Though representing social classes and political stances, these characters still carry their own psychological inclinations, which preclude objective reasoning and bring them close to the myth.[18] Paulo's poetic discourse, in *Land in Trance,* rather than justifying his contradictory political actions, unveils his oedipal love-hate relationship with the tyrant Díaz, as well as his dependence on Sara and Silvia. He worships Díaz as the "God of my youth", a man who acts both as father figure and intellectual mentor.

Whenever in crisis, he delivers himself to alcohol-fuelled orgies in the company of Eldorado's magnates. The constant states of trance thus produced send him back to religion and the vision of politics as a matter of "faith" ("The naivety of faith!", he exclaims), rather than conviction. Paulo literally expresses his disdain for reason, proclaiming that he "prefers the madness of Porfírio Díaz".

In both films, revolution rather than battles and carnage staged with troops is suggested through synecdochic procedures: a gun, carried by one single revolutionary character, stands for an entire army, whereas the mere sound of shots represents whole battles. Xavier talks about the gun as fetish in *Land in Trance,* because we never really see any result of its use.[19]

Also in *I Am Cuba* the country is personified through a female voice-over narrator. In a way not dissimilar to Paulo's poetic voice-over in *Land in Trance,* Cuba's female voice recites a poem about the country which regularly punctuates the film with its chorus "Soy Cuba", without ever referring to any real political facts in present-day Cuba. A newsreel footage briefly showing the dictator Fulgencio Batista in a drive-in cinema is only there to cause the rebel students to set fire to the giant screen.

The process of personifying the country as a woman is not dissimilar from devices normally used in nationalist narratives. As Susan Hayward notes, "The nation pretends to be gender-neutral (in that it purports to dissolve difference) and yet the woman's body is closely aligned/identified with nationalist discourses. We fight and die for our mother-nation. [...] the colonised referred to

---

[18] See, in this respect, Xavier, *Allegories of Underdevelopment: Aesthetics and Politics in Modern Brazilian Cinema,* p. 69.

[19] Xavier, *Allegories of Underdevelopment: Aesthetics and Politics in Modern Brazilian Cinema,* p. 69.

the colonising country as mother-country. When 'she' is invaded by the enemy, she is 'raped'."[20] Also in *I Am Cuba* colonial domination is presented from the outset as the invasion of a virgin land. Sexual metaphors are employed throughout the film, though no direct allusion to rape is made. The camera seems to be constantly diving into and penetrating this woman-country from above or outside, and investigating its interior with a foreign, fascinated gaze.

Cuba's female voice echoes that of the character Maria/Betty, who, though not actually raped, is torn between two opposing forces. Incarnating the sanctified prostitute, a mixture of the Christian myths of Virgin Mary and Mary Magdalene, she is divided between the attraction of money, brought in by the rich Americans, and the true love of her countryman, which is blessed by the church. This causes her to fall into a trance induced by jazz, the African wooden idols and alcohol in the nightclub scene.

Maria/Betty is reminiscent of another mythical Maria, that of *Metropolis*, by Fritz Lang (1926), in which the character is not only a double but a multiple woman, a true allegory encapsulating several narratives. She is the Christian salvation for the poor, but also the evil robot working for the Lord of Metropolis. Moreover, she is the copy of the latter's deceased wife, hence the mother of his son who is in love with her, which completes the Oedipal triangulation. Maria, the robot, is portrayed as the reverse of the virgin, the whore, who dances topless in the nightclub for a horde of lustful men. Later she is carried on the men's shoulders, screaming: "let's watch the world going to hell".

In *I Am Cuba,* alongside the Christian myths of the virgin and the prostitute, there is a widespread use of the cross in another synecdochic procedure, which stands for the church and religion as a whole. Maria/Betty is constantly holding her pendant crucifix, a token from her Cuban boyfriend who proposed to her in front of the cathedral. Her American lover, on the other hand, is a crucifix collector who, after his night of love with Betty, takes away her pendant, thus suggesting the end to Maria's hopes of a normal marriage.

[20] Susan Hayward, "Framing National Cinemas", in Mette Hjort and Scott Mackenzie, *Cinema and Nation* (London/New York: Routledge, 2002), pp. 97ff.

In *Land in Trance,* Porfírio Díaz is constantly grasping an enormous cross to signal his allegiance to God and attachment to power. Here, Christian imagery is viewed under a critical light which is reminiscent of Eisenstein's use of the same symbolism in *The Battleship Potemkin.* The cross also reflects the torn state of the characters, whose torments never find a resolution. As in the endless massacre on the steps of Odessa, in Eisenstein, Paulo's agony is stretched from the beginning to the end of the film. In Robert Stam's words, "Paulo's death, co-extensive with the film, recalls the protracted agonies of opera, where people die eloquently, interminably, and in full voice".[21]

Lack of resolution is typical of intermediary characters, who are constantly agonising between opposing forces. Paulo, the poet, is always between two individuals whom he simultaneously loves and hates. He is also a journalist, a media man, who uses the power of the press to favour or destroy politicians, depending on his oscillating moods. In a male-oriented world, where intellectual and revolutionary roles are carried out by men, the intellectualised, revolutionary woman is also turned into a go-between, and it is interesting to observe how both *Land in Trance* and *I Am Cuba* arrived at similar aesthetic results to represent her social position, which is just a little more than that of a secretary. Sara, the mother figure, whom Paulo reveres and depends on, is introduced to us as "the powerful woman behind the man", as she takes notes of Vieira's resignation speech. The triangular composition is achieved here with Sara between Vieira and Paulo, who strongly opposes Vieira's resignation.

In *I Am Cuba,* Enrique rushes to his university when he hears the false rumour of Fidel Castro's death. There, he meets the head of the students' union, who dictates a letter to a female student, quite in the same way, ignoring Enrique's clamour for immediate action against the repressive forces.

The land as architecture and the architecture of power

Especially in *I Am Cuba,* but also in *Land in Trance,* anti-realism approaches expressionism. In both films, the subjective camera,

[21] Stam, "Land in Anguish", p. 156.

often hand-held, is used to convey the characters' disturbed minds, as in the scene of Enrique's death, in *I Am Cuba,* when the image blurs like an abstract painting. Through the projection of the character's inner feelings, the subjective camera conveys a world in dissolution. Close-ups are used to deform faces and turn smiles into grotesque frowns, as in the nightclub scene in *I Am Cuba,* and the orgiastic parties in *Land in Trance.*

A subjective point of hearing is used in both films to produce distortions. The soundtrack frequently overlaps all sorts of incomprehensible noises, such as screams, opera fragments and machine gun shots, in *Land in Trance.* In *I Am Cuba,* the sound often derives from the characters' mental hearing, as they are plagued by recollections such as those of gunshots, an old man's voice singing to the sound of his guitar, barking dogs or a pounding mortar. Also in this film, the camera's constant plunging into the interior of things, such as the spectacular sequence-shot that descends along a high-rise to the inside of a swimming pool, suggests the vertigo of the fall and death. A similar effect is produced when Betty accepts that the foreigner penetrates her interior realms, which are tight, stuffy and wet. The ceiling of her house is too low, forcing her American client to lower his head; the floor is sloping; all is precarious and provisional, suggesting the disequilibrium, discomfort and instability of an expressionist setting.

The architecture in both films is also personified and used to express class struggle. Stairs, as in Eisenstein (Odessa, in *Potemkin*) or Fritz Lang (*Metropolis*), are a favourite trope through which ornamental masses circulate between upper and lower levels. In *Land in Trance,* palace staircases, terraces and high-rises are the elevated site of the powerful, whereas the chaotic masses crawl in the obscure depths. In *I Am Cuba,* faith in revolution is expressed through the clear spaces and straight lines of modern architecture, with geometric staircases which endlessly unfold while leading the masses to death for the motherland and the ensuing victory of revolution.

Land in Trance's disillusionment sends us back to the baroque, the curve, the circle and excess, whereas the straight line in *I Am Cuba* is the teleology that resolves the chaos. Though they arrive at different results, both films work on a purely symbolic level, where, free from the constraints of realism, the idea of revolution can be conveyed.

Conclusion

The anti-realist stance in both films transfers the site of revolution from its real settings to the film form. *Land in Trance* denies effectiveness to existing political proposals, centred on the national question, proposing instead the breaking of national and cultural boundaries. Rather than explaining the specific Brazilian case, it questions the role of the intellectual, including the one behind the camera, and suggests that revolution in art can only derive from the artist's despair and doubts that lead to the state of trance. The composer and singer Caetano Veloso asserts that the artistic movement Tropicália would not have existed were it not for the impact caused by *Land in Trance*. For him, the film revealed "unconscious aspects of [the Brazilian] reality" and offered the means for his own breaking of boundaries between the national and the foreign, and between high and popular culture.[22]

In a similar manner, *I Am Cuba* conveys little information on the Cuban revolution itself, and its propagandistic aims are as ineffective today as they were at the time the film was made. But it is a revolution in itself. "Each scene we filmed was like a battle, a combat, as if we were preparing a small revolution", says Sacha Calzatti in *Soy Cuba – The Siberian Mammoth*. And indeed this gigantic super-production, whose shooting, animated by obsessive perfectionism, stretched over two years, is a monument to the human capacity of invention and transformation. Because it attaches little value to the mere document, it was despised and forgotten both in Cuba and the USSR after just a few screenings, and consequently excluded from film history for several decades. A filmmaker such as Martin Scorsese, who, together with Francis Ford Coppola, was responsible for its relaunch in the early 1990s, believes that he would have done a different kind of cinema had he been able to watch *I Am Cuba* in the early 1960s. In Scorsese's opinion, the entire history of cinema since the masking of *I am*

---

[22] Caetano Veloso, *Verdade tropical* (São Paulo: Companhia das Letras, 1997), p. 99ff.

Cuba would have been different if the film had been duly shown at its time.[23]

Passion for cinema is, in effect, the very essence of *Land in Trance* and *I Am Cuba,* allowing identification through cinephilia, rather than through manipulation and illusionistic catharsis. In a fascinating essay, Many Ann Doane connects cinephilia to indexicality or cinema's material link with the world, saying: "what cinephilia names is the moment when the contingent takes on meaning. [...] The cinephile maintains a certain belief, an investment in the graspability of the asystematic, the contingent, for which the cinema is the privileged vehicle".[24] Indeed, both films, while attesting to the international circulation of cinematic images, provide the living proof of the reality of the medium.

[23] Martin Scorsese, Interview in the extras of the DVD of *I Am Cuba* (Mr Bongo Films, 2006).
[24] Mary Ann Doane, "The Object of Theory", in Ivone Margulies (ed.), *Rites of Realism – Essays on Corporeal Cinema* (Durham, NC/London: Duke University Press, 2003), pp. 83-84.

Music, Literature and Cinema: a Comparative Approach to the Aesthetics of Death in *Tous les matins du monde*[1]

Germán Gil-Curiel
University of Nottingham Ningbo, China

To Gerardo and Gabriel

Je suis le Ténébreux,—le Veuf,—l'Inconsolé,
Le Prince d'Aquitaine à la Tour abolie :
Ma seule Étoile est morte,—et mon luth constellé
Porte le Soleil noir de la Mélancolie.
- Gérard de Nerval, "El Desdichado", in *Les Chimères.*[2]

—Yo soy, dijo la muerte, tu verdadera madre.
La que te trajo al mundo te trajo a mis brazos para siempre.
Te hablé y tú me oías, y me llamabas tierra.

- Jaime Sabines, in "El poeta y la muerte".[3]

Within the framework of the philosophy of music and from the perspective of a comparative methodology, this paper explores some of the metaphysical features that constitute the specificity of an aesthetics of death in Pascal Quignard's novel *Tous les matins du monde* and the cinematic adaptation of that novel by Alain Corneau. And in doing so, how the narrative discourses in the literary, musical and cinematographic domains merge in both the novel and the film, through music. Quignard's text recreates the historical actuality of Sainte Colombe's life and his relationship

---

[1] I would like to thank Lúcia Nagib for reading an earlier version of this text and providing thoughtful comments and suggestions.
[2] "I am the Dark, —the Widowed, —the Unconsoled,/The Prince of Aquitania of the ruined Tower:/My only Star is dead, — and my starred lute/Bears the black Sun of Melancholy". From "The Outcast" in Stanley Burnshaw, (ed.), *The Poem Itself* (Arkansas: University of Arkansas Press, 1995), p. 2.
[3] "I am, said Death, your true mother. The one who brought you to the world, brought you into my arms for ever. I talked to you and you heard me, and you called me Earth." ("The Poet and Death"). Jaime Sabines, *Poesía, Nuevo Recuento de Poemas* (México: Joaquín Mortiz, 1986), p. 149.

with his pupil Marin Marais, in a free interpretation.[4] This enquiry, aesthetical and metaphysical, deals with two essential motifs in Quignard's novel and Corneau's homonymous film: the reunion and the separation of the *amants* in the context of two different narrations. Whereas the former occurs in the context of the return of the dead from the beyond – as, when playing his viol, Sainte Colombe feels the presence of this dead wife — the latter takes place through a suicide — this time Sainte Colombe's daughter who takes her own life as the result of a failed love affair with Marin Marais, her father's pupil.

The idea that the various arts have common properties and that they are susceptible to being analysed by means of a common language has recently gained increasing credence.[5] In *Tous les matins du monde* — a context for a blurring of boundaries between the supposedly separate, artistic realms of literature, cinema and music — three different aesthetical experiences converge; each merging with the other to become one through a creative interaction of mixed associations.[6] In Quignard's novel, the scenes concerning Madame de Sainte Colombe's return from the beyond and Madeleine's and Marin Marais's separation preceding her suicide take place through a prose of concentrated sobriety and simplicity. Its unusual strength is based too in the nature of both transcendental events that have slowly but inexorably been developed throughout the novel. On the other hand, in Corneau's film, which for the most part follows the novel's structure accurately, the force of contained passions is portrayed in both scenes by means of a very detailed description of the character's faces, the creation of interior spaces, landscapes, silent

---

[4] Written by Pascal Quignard and published in 1991, *Tous les matins du monde* was adapted for the screen by Alain Corneau the same year. The film was scripted by Pascal Quignard, with music directed and performed by Jordi Savall. Pascal Quignard, *Tous les Matins du Monde* (Barcelona: Gallimard, 1991).

[5] Inasmuch as it entails the synthesis of essential cultural values, musical discourse is a philosophical statement, in spite of its inherent resistance to interpretation.

[6] This is an idea also put forward in the film itself: for instance, on mentioning how music and painting relate to each other, at some point Sainte Colombe compares the viol's bow with the painter's brush.

atmospheres of peace and silence and chiaroscuros — all this against the background of a slowly phrasing viol. Like Sainte Colombe's intimist aesthetics, Alain Corneau's cinema is created on the basis of innermost thoughts and feelings.

In this paper, I first briefly sketch out the context and basic plot of both the film and the novel, and then analyse how the opposition between the two musicians' lives, linked by means of death, merge with music to become a single aesthetic experience, partaking of and inseparable from word, image and sound.

The musicians

Through traditional links between the monarchy and music reinforced by the personal taste of the sovereigns, during the seventeenth century the court of Versailles became one of the main musical centres of Europe. French music from the *Grand Siècle* is the legacy of a long tradition and the fruit of a monopolising will. Royal power, through its dance and music academies, exerted an absolute control over musical production and over musicians belonging to the trade, chorus or specialised institutions. According to the canon, a host of musicians should play for the King. Among them was Marin Marais, who played from the age of twenty in Jean-Baptiste Lully's orchestra. But about Monsieur de Sainte Colombe, there is little to say. Other than a few scant details, little is known about him. This may be due to the lack of interest in fame and fortune he always displayed. Be that as it may, enough information is conveyed in both the novel and the film to make sense of his character.

Monsieur de Sainte Colombe is a man who lives absorbed by the "intact memory" of his wife. After her death, upon which he composes the *Tombeau des Regrets*, he renounces mundane satisfactions, social and material affairs, as well as all things he used to love the most on earth, such as — put both in writing and on screen — flowers, pastries, rolled scores, kites, faces, pewter plates and wine. A circumspect, irascible man, but loving of his two daughters Madeleine and Toinette, the musician abandons himself to states of painful consciousness arising from the loss of his wife. Then, he locks himself up in a country cottage for years where he plays for up to fifteen hours a day, absorbed in his music and his compositions, strengthened by amorous devotion to the memories of his beloved wife.

Given his profoundly intimate conception of the musical art; a conception that separates him from the political and the social matters of life, he bluntly and repeatedly refuses to play before the King and his Court. When Monsieur Caignet, a viol player in the Court, comes to tell Moinseur de Sainte Colombe that the King wishes to listen to his performance, he does not hesitate in expressing his contempt for the world of the Court, and his categorical refusal to join in with the herd of musicians, dazzled by Versailles' splendour, who play to rejoice his Majesty's ear. "Je suis si sauvage, Monsieur, que je pense que je n'appartiens qu'à moi-même",[7] he replies in an outburst of fury. The relation between the artist and the Court reaches its worst point when Abbot Mathieu, tries to dissuade the outrageous revolt of this *homme sauvage* who dares to despise the wealth, luxury and glory offered to him by his Majesty. The musician categorically replies to him:

Je préfère la lumière du couchant sur mes mains à l'or qu'elle me propose. Je préfère mes vêtements de drap à vos perruques in-folio. Je préfère mes poules aux violons du roi et mes porcs à vous-mêmes.[8]

By contrast, Marin Marais' relentless ambition to achieve glory and wealth in the Court — since he had been from an early age seduced by the idea of becoming a famous viol player — has the following consequences: firstly, having been rejected by his mentor Sainte Colombe for playing before the King — a fact that will enable him to become a King's musician later on — Marin Marais is prevented from coming to Bièvre, where Sainte Colombe lives; and secondly, dazzled by the court's splendour, he will abandon Sainte Colombe's elder daughter Madeleine, with whom he has been having a relationship. Marin Marais' ambitions reaffirm his

---

[7] "I am such a savage, Sir, that I believe I belong only to myself." Quignard, *Tous les matins du monde*, p. 26.

[8] "I prefer the twilight on my hands to the gold that he proposes. I prefer my woollen clothes to your wigs in-folio. I prefer my hens to the king's violins and my pigs to yourselves" (Quignard, *Tous les matins du monde*, pp. 29-30).

mentor's project by means of the contrast between his desire to become a famous musician and Sainte Colombe's indifference to the Court.

Music and death

The antagonism between both musicians is transposed onto a purely aesthetic level through two transcendental motifs: resurrection and death. The return from the beyond opposes the voluntary departure for the beyond. Indeed, the essential opposition, death and life, is subverted. While Madelaine commits suicide, late Madame de Sainte Colombe comes back from the beyond. Thus bound up with the theme of death and caused by the strong feelings, emotions and consuming passions, both transcendental events share the same fatal impossibility of the fulfilment of love: a ghost in love coming from the beyond during a piece of music, and an actual suicide in love, departing for the beyond. Indeed, both extreme experiences are transferred to a deeper dimension of internalisation thanks to two moving and ineffable pieces of music: *Les Pleurs* by Sainte Colombe and *La Rêveuse* by Marin Marais, respectively.[9] In Quignard's novel and Corneau's film, music and death are inextricable. While Sainte Colombe selects a *Tombeau* as his preferred musical form — an instrumental structure composed by a musician in memory of a master, mentor or, in this case, a friend — Marin Marais's piece, to the absent beloved woman, has the form of an air.[10]

[9] Sainte Colombe, *Les Pleurs* ("The Sorrows"), Jordi Savall, version for viol solo; Marin Marais, *La Rêveuse* ("The Dreaming Girl"), 4th book of "Pièces de viole"; Jordi Savall (bass viol), Pierre Hantaï (clavichord), Rolf Lislevand (theorbo).

[10] The former takes the cadence of a deep and slow dance, very close to an *allemande*; given its instrumental nature. It is different from other genres of *Déplorations*, which are vocal. The *Tombeau des Regrets*, to which the piece *Les Pleurs* belongs, is in D minor, a low tonality that quite fits the narrative discourse of a funerary prayer. As for the *Rêveuse* by Marin Marais, a fragment of the 4° book (1717), it has the character of an elegy and it belongs to the "aisées, chantantes et peu chargées d'accords" group of pieces. This work has the structure of an *air*, a structure that enjoyed considerable prestige in France during the seventeenth and the eighteenth centuries.

Musically, the motifs of reunion and separation resonate with the categories of tonality, tempo and cadence. Tonality being, in musical terms, the dominance of a note which does not lose its function as the fundamental element in the structure despite the modulations that may appear in a given piece; and which is transposed, in literary and cinematographic discourses, into an essential focal point, as if it were the dominant colour in a painting. In *Tous les matins du monde*, in both the novel and the film, this tonality corresponds to the fundamental motif of death, inasmuch as the many meanings flowing from reunion and the separation concern the ontological problem of the idea of death. The tonality on the screen is realised by means of shadows, chiaroscuro and darkness, at the very moment in which the two scenes dealt with here are unfolded. Musically, this motif is constructed by the dominance of the minor mode in the tonality of both pieces. These elements contribute to the creation of an atmosphere of hopelessness, desolation, detachment and loneliness, which is also developed in the novel.

Regarding the *tempi* of these pieces of music, *Les Pleurs* and *La Rêveuse*, it is interesting to note that rather than a musical line developing chronologically over time, we listen to a static musical discourse. This gives the impression that those notes, without being disturbed by the laws of movement, float, as it were, in an empty, timeless space. Again, this still atmosphere determines — and is determined by — the ontological notion of the impermanence of beings. Moreover, it corresponds, in the literary and cinematographic aesthetic realms, to the low voices and the whispers, the glimpses, the sighs and the silences of both scenes, held as they are on the threshold of death. Indeed, the vision of time incorporated into Western music corresponds to the traditional Christian cosmology: time begins with a decisive act of creation and it advances, straightforwardly, towards a final, apocalyptic event.[11]

In the sense of rise and the fall of the musical narration, cadence also constructs a contained, quiet and peaceful tension during these scenes. Musical narrative *talks*, so to speak, and words falls silent. "La musique est simplement là pour parler de ce dont la

---

[11] On the concept of musical tempo, see Jonathan D. Kramer, "New Temporalities", in *Critical Inquiry* 7, 1981, pp. 549-52.

parole ne peut parler. En ce sens elle n'est pas tout à fait humaine", tells the master to his disciple later.[12] During these emotional instants, the silent gestures of characters seen on the screen amalgamate with the strong and subtle pulse of the music; and through this profoundly intimate state, the ineffable is suggested.

Death

The return from the beyond is one of the cornerstones of a literature of the supernatural framed within the aesthetics of death. In a very enigmatic way, the act of facing death turns its witnesses into special, extraordinary beings. Representatives of this transgression such as dreamers, clairvoyants and visionaries are socially excluded; protagonists deeply individualised and differentiated from others. Obsessed with and fascinated by death, they are prone to falling into aberrant states as varied as their inner nature: meditation, detachment, melancholy, nostalgia, hallucinations, strong emotions and perturbations such as delirium tremens and intangible terror. The recurrence, intensity and length of time of these psychic, transitory moments depends on each particular case. Ghostly presences might project a more transcendental meaning. Paradoxically, a narrative dealing with the representation of death somehow turns into a transcendental reflection on the significance of life.

To Marcel Schneider, the supernatural in literature is an act of transgression against the *status quo*. It also has the function of exorcising our inner fears. He contends that the fantastic:

> ne nous décharge pas de notre misère, mais il en émousse les aiguillons en exorcisant nos démons turbulents. Grâce à lui, nous pouvons libérer nos désirs les plus avides, nos rêves les plus tenaces et donner corps à notre espérance.[13]

---

[12] "Music is there simply to speak about that which word cannot express. In this sense, music is not wholly human" (Quignard, *Tous les matins du monde*, p. 113).

[13] "It does not take the burden of our misery away, but it blunts down its stings exorcising our tempestuous demons. Thanks to it, we can liberate

According to Michel Guiomar's assertions about the aesthetics of death, "Le Fantastique est le lieu où nous affrontons notre propre conception de la Mort pour la domineer."[14] The immediate effects of this rupture are: the deployment of a particular uncanny created by the presence of death and a tendency towards a systematic transgression by bringing about facts that escape comprehension. In *Tous les matins du monde*, the return of the spectre is created through precarious and uncertain moments giving rise to another dimension that makes reality crumble. Here, music and the idea of death merge to construct a deep internalisation dealing with the search for meaning.

The Scenes

In the novel, in his cottage, through the enigmatic dimension of written word, we can *listen* to the gloomy lament of the *Tombeau des Regrets* which, in a sort of state of grace, makes the impossible possible: the ultimate transgression, that of the return from among the dead:

> Tandis que le chant montait, près de la porte une femme très pâle apparut qui lui souriait tout en posant le doigt sur son sourire en signe qu'elle ne parlerait pas et qu'il ne se dérangeât pas de ce qu'il était en train de faire. Elle contourna en silence le pupitre de Monsieur de Sainte Colombe. Elle s'assit sur le coffre à musique qui était dans le coin auprès de la table et du flacon de vin et elle l'écouta.[15]

our most avid desires, our most tenacious dreams and materialise our hope." Marcel Schneider, *La littérature fantastique en France* (Paris: Fayard, 1964) p. 409.

[14] "The fantastic is a continuum, an irrepressible protestation against what is, against the created world and the life one leads there." Michel Guiomar, *Principes D'une Esthétique de la Mort* (Paris, Jose Corti, 1967), p. 371.

[15] "As the melody rose, near the door a very pale woman appeared, smiling at him and indicating by her finger that she would not speak, so that he would not be disturbed in what he was doing. She walked silently around the music stand of Monsieur de Sainte Colombe. She sat down on the trunk of music which was in the corner near the table and the

In the film, during this scene the camera captures the actions that prepare the apparition of the spectre of Madame de Sainte Colombe: the musician's return to the cottage, the wine he drinks, his gesture when he renounces reading music, his subtle movements when performing the piece, his tears. From that moment on, deep meanings in the manner of Baudelaire's "Recueillement" are projected through his gestures and his appearance. The musician's face in the foreground, then that of his beloved wife, become a silent language expressing the deepest emotions of the human condition, brought together in a conjunction in which *Eros* and *Thanatos* eternally consume each other. Needless to say, this is made possible thanks to music.

After Marin Marais's last visit to Bièvre, literary and cinematographic narratives and music work together to create an environment of renouncement and detachment, together announcing Madeleine's suicide. While the reunion of the lovers, a coming back from the beyond, is paradoxically the projection of a powerful vital energy, Madeleine's unreciprocated love, leading to her death, is a renunciation of life. In Quignard's novel, acquiescing to Toinette's plea to go and see her sister, given the deterioration of her physical and mental health, Marais has to quit Versailles. During his last visit to the Bièvre he is forced to face the devastation his abandonment has wrought on Mademoiselle de Sainte Colombe. Once again, music plays a key role in the climax of this scene. Upon the sick woman's request, Marin Marais plays la *Rêveuse*, an *air* that synthesises the loneliness and desperation of the woman through its slow and painful phrasing, giving a sensation as if the soul shivered before the weight of the memory of the beloved's body, hopelessly trying to recover from a fatal fall. *La Rêveuse* reflects all of Madeleine's profound misery, as faithfully as a mirror showing her own image: a face distorted by rancour, despair and starvation, and her renouncement of life, which it announces with its mysterious cadence.

In Corneau's film, the camera focuses on the fissures that separate the erstwhile lovers: Marin Marais's magnificent aspect, as well as his self-confident air, contrast with the asphyxiating atmosphere of the ailing woman's room, her skeletal body, her

---

bottle of wine and she listened" (Quignard, *Tous les matins du monde,* pp. 36-37).

trembling hands, her cadaverous face, her contained rancour. In a soft and harsh voice she urges the musician to play *La Rêveuse*. In the novel, after his final departure preparations for the suicide are made silently, interrupted only by Madeleine sighing: "Elle soufflait comme si les trois quarts du souffle dont elle disposait étaient taris."[16] In the film, Mademoiselle de Sainte Colombe prepares to die on the notes of such a melancholic music. The effect in both circumstances could hardly be more poetic and deeply moving.

Once the suicide has taken place in the film, the spectator sees Madeleine's hanging legs in the foreground, while in the background there is the fading image of the dead woman's viol shape leaning on the room's wall. Here, Marin Marais has not only betrayed love, but also art. According to Sainte Colombe's aesthetical principles, art and passion —"Passion", that is to say Life—, are forever one and the same thing.

Conclusion

Foucault deals with the problem of modernity on the basis of the definition of Baudelaire, who conceived of modernity as "the ephemeral, the fleeting and the contingent". According to this idea, modern man is he who adopts a specific attitude before the discontinuity of time, consisting in "recapturing something that is not beyond the present instant, nor behind it, but within it".[17] On this basis, Foucault proposes the relation we ought to have with ourselves should be one of aesthetic creation:

> From the idea that the self is not given to us, I think that there is only one practical consequence: we have to create ourselves as a work of art [...]. We should not have to refer the creative activity of somebody to the kind of relation he has to himself, but should relate the kind of relation one has to oneself to creative activity.[18]

Sainte Colombe"s experience overcomes a search for his past in

---

[16] "She puffed as if she were out of the breath." Quignard, *Tous les matins du monde*, pp. 105-106.

[17] Michel Foucault, "What is Enlightenment?", in Paul Rabinow (ed.), *The Foucault Reader* (London: Penguin, 1991), p. 39.

[18] Foucault, "What is Enlightenment?", p. 35.

the loneliness of his memories and his melancholy. Indeed, the realisation of Sainte Colombe's aesthetic project, an "ascetic elaboration of the self", as it would be put by Foucault, is only possible by means of a profound individuality. Similarly to Gérard de Nerval's poetical project comprising the whole meaning of life-death, Sainte Colombe's search points to the importance of conceiving passionate existence as a way to access a superior truth, beyond the platitudes of this world.

Within the framework of the aesthetics of death, "this solitary, gifted with an active imagination, ceaselessly journeying across the great human desert",[19] invents himself through an adventure that humanises him. This exceptional man is initiated in the truth that "Tous les matins du monde sont sans retour"[20] — and makes of his body, his behaviour, his feelings and passions, of his very existence, a work of art.[21]

[19] Foucault, "What is Enlightenment?", p. 40.
[20] "Each day dawns but once."
[21] Foucault, "What is Enlightenment?", pp. 41-42.

**Challenging the Territorial Boundaries of the Nation:
Chicanos on Mexican Film in the 1990s**

Armida de la Garza
University of Nottingham Ningbo, China

Who are the Mexican people? Traditionally, they are taken to be those descendents of the Spanish conquerors and the Indians, and are thus called *mestizos*; hybridity being the very essence of *Mexicanity* itself. To distinguish Mexicans from other Latin Americans, "the Aztecs" are often taken as shorthand for the various indigenous peoples that inhabited the Americas in the central region of what today is Mexico before the arrival of the Spaniards. This view of a supposedly distinctive Mexican ethnicity based on the uniqueness of its indigenous origins is, together with the Spanish dialects spoken there and the syncretic Catholic religion embraced by the vast majority of the population, the basis of the national identity. In addition, the white Protestant dominated, English-speaking northern neighbour further enhanced Mexican identity through difference, clearly establishing the limits, physical as well as symbolic, of the country, especially after the invasion in 1847 which severed half the Mexican land.

This is of course a discursive construction, since "hybridity" is always already there. It was at the heart of the supposedly pure and homogeneous "Spaniards" as well as "the Indians". But nonetheless, from the revolution until the 1990s, the facts outlined above were woven together into a narrative that provided the ideological basis for the *Partido Revolucionario Institucional* (PRI), the single party that dominated Mexican politics for the best part of the 20th century, to remain in power. Essentially, a positive connotation was given to the purported hybridity of Mexicans, characterising them as the healthier, stronger product of a pool of genes instead of the "half breed" that had been prevalent before, and policies of assimilation were thoroughly pursued that would turn the remaining indigenous minorities into cultural mestizos.[1]

---

[1] Minna Stern, "From Mestizophilia to Biotypology: Racialization and Science in Mexico, 1920-1960" in Thomas Holt, Nancy P. Appelbaum, Anne S. Macpherson and Karin A. Rosemblatt (eds.), *Race and Nation in*

"The Indians" would from then on have the role of ancestors, having existed in a mythical Golden Age the national destiny would one day return the people to. As a result, there was a strong sense of who the national "we" were, and the government gained legitimacy, inasmuch as it belonged to this "we". A strong sense of loyalty to the group was cultivated, partly through pride in the cultural values that were different from those of the United States, especially the centrality of the family unit and traditions. The international context in which all this took place was appropriate for this revolutionary nationalism to flourish, since especially after the Second World War decolonisation was taking place and the nation state was officially endorsed in discourses on world politics.

Not surprisingly, Chicanos, those Mexican immigrants who settled in the United States, at the time referred to, derogatorily, as "pochos", were more often than not ignored in cultural representations of the nation such as national cinema, and when they were dealt with at all, they were duly portrayed as pitiful creatures at best and outright traitors at worst. Simultaneously claiming the Mexican identity and the American identity that was, until the 1990s, its discursive opposite, Chicanos questioned the fit between the political and the territorial unit that nationalism struggles to create. The undecidability of the Chicano identity exposed the contingency of the hegemonic meaning of *Mexicanidad*. Thus, from Miguel Contreras Torres' *El Hombre sin Patria/The Man without a Fatherland* (1922), and through films with titles such as *Los Desarraigados/ The Uprooted* (1958) and *Espaldas Mojadas/Wetbacks* (1954), Mexican cinema consistently conveyed three messages regarding Mexicans in the United States and their experience. First of all, there were those stories of people who, as put by David Maciel, crossed the Rio Bravo "to the land of the dollars in search of an illusive El Dorado", only to suffer unspeakable misfortune.[2] Then there were those films which showed the pocho to be a sort of fake Mexican, a threat to the

---

Modern Latin America (Chapel Hill: University of North Carolina, 2003), p. 190.

[2] David Maciel,. "Pochos and Other Extremes in Mexican Cinema, or El Cine Mexicano se va de Bracero, 1922-1963" in Chon A. Noriega (ed.), *Chicanos and Film: Representation and Resistance* (Minneapolis: The University of Minnesota Press, 1992), p. 110.

national culture who would, as it were, dilute or contaminate *Mexicanidad* through the influence of the American culture of which he or she had become a bearer. And occasionally, a few films did celebrate not so much the immigrants, but those Mexicans who had fought in the 1847 war against the United States to preserve their land.

Representations of Mexican emigrants were therefore overwhelmingly negative. The only exceptions to these depictions were the ones put forward by Chicano directors themselves, very much in the minority, and more importantly, regarded in Mexico as American. In the words of Emilio García-Riera in 1990, "we must insist that when we refer to Chicano cinema we mean a foreign cinema, a part of the North American cinema that is in no way an offshoot of Mexican cinema. On the contrary, Chicano cinema is a rival to Mexican cinema, a powerful competitor of which Mexican cinema must beware."[3] This assessment was made despite the fact that the Mexican government provided the funding for some of the Chicano production.

During the 1990s however, deep changes took place in world politics and in Mexico as well. The Soviet Union collapsed and discourses of globalisation began to replace the former revolutionary nationalism. Aspirations to autarchy were abandoned and dependence for trade on the United States, formerly regarded as an obstacle to be overcome, was instead viewed as access to the American market, a unique opportunity for Mexico to grow via economic integration through the North American Free Trade Agreement (NAFTA), including the liberalisation of the film industry. To this end, a type of forward-looking, modernising national identity, that would seek fulfilment in a promised future rather than in a bygone Golden Age, was promoted.

Already in 1988 it was hoped that NAFTA would lead, through spill over, to the creation of a Union, with open borders in exchange for oil, gas and electricity. Academic and later Minister of Foreign Affairs Jorge Castañeda, put it as follows: "With new leadership, the moment is ripe to consider a package deal that would involve major concessions and demands by both nations in

[3] Emilio García-Riera, *México Visto por el Cine Extranjero, 1970-1988* (México D.F.: Era Universidad de Guadalajara, 1990), vol. 5, p. 141 (present author's translation).

trade, energy, intelligence and security, debt, capital flight and immigration."[4] In 1995 a law allowing dual nationality for Mexican citizens was passed. At the national university, the Centre for Research on North America broadened its scope to include Mexico. By 1999, Vicente Fox, then a presidential candidate, emphasised the proposed creation of institutions for the welfare of migrants, whom he cast as heroes, enthusiastically encouraging Mexicans to, like them, "dream the American dream". Members of Parliament to represent migrants were appointed in Zacatecas, one of the key sending states, and were proposed in other states as well. Even CNN (Cable News Network) weather forecasts shown in Mexico included Mexican cities when telling the forecast for the US. The term *pocho* was dropped in favour of the more positive *Chicano*.[5] Could it be that Mexico's future economic success would be in this North American region, and Mexican identity accordingly redefined? As the nearly thirty million American citizens of Mexican ancestry have now made the national identity "inherently diasporic",[6] could the Chicano become the new discursively constructed *hybrid* basis for the nation, so to speak? Here I will discuss two of the only three Mexican films made in this decade explicitly dealing with the issue, as well as representations of Mexican emigrants in Border Cinema over the same period, to offer an interpretation on whether negotiations of the national identity on cinema matched the efforts made in other fields of cultural production.[7]

Let us start with a brief comment on *Como Agua para Chocolate*. Although not dealing specifically with migrants, Alfonso Arau's famous film of 1991 seemed to answer the question of a possible regional identity with an emphatic "yes". While it is true that, as Barbara Tenenbaum observed, Tita could not and did not marry

---

[4] Jorge Castañeda and Robert A. Pastor, *Limits to Friendship: the United States and Mexico* (New York: Alfred A. Knopf, 1988), p. 370.
[5] Armida de la Garza, *Mexico on Film: National Identity and International Relations* (Bury St Edmonds: Arena, 2006), pp. 126-133.
[6] Geffrey Kantaris, "Cinema and Urbanías: Translocal Identities in Contemporary Mexican Film" in *Bulletin of Latin American Research* 24, 4 (Oxford: Blackwell, 2006), p. 521.
[7] The third film, not discussed in this paper, is *Bajo California: en el límite del Tiempo* (1998), by Carlos Bolado.

the American doctor, for it would have amounted to "Mexico being conquered again", her niece Esperanza does indeed marry the doctor's son, leaving integration to the new generation. This matched other gendered representations of the relation between Mexico and the United States in newspapers and academic discourse, such as Sidney Weintraub's book entitled *A Marriage of Convenience: Relations between Mexico and the United States* (1999).[8] But more importantly, one of the reasons *Como Agua para Chocolate* was so successful in the United States is without doubt the fact that the type of romanticised Mexico presented there struck a chord with the many conservative and religious audiences in the United States, who, to quote Tenenbaum again found "there is something alluring…about a solid family tradition, according to which children live at home until marriage and do not move so far away they cannot come back for Sunday dinner every week".[9] Despite the huge economic and political differences between Mexico and the United States, *Como Agua* thus managed to portray points of convergence: similarities in the key social values held. Again, this conforms to the findings of Ronald Inglehart's survey on civic culture, published in 1996 as "The North American Trajectory: Cultural, Economic and Political Ties Among the United States, Canada and Mexico",[10] where he concludes there are more similarities in terms of conservative social values between Mexico and the US than between the US and other members of the so-called West. Further, his research also found a kind of generation gap between the opinions of adults and the younger generations in Mexico as regards the United States; the latter holding much more favourable views.

Let us discuss now the first of the films that did engage with the issue of migration. In 1993, in a French, Canadian and Mexican

---

[8] Sidney Weintraub, *A Marriage of Convenience: Relations between Mexico and the United States*, (New York: Oxford University Press, 1999).

[9] Barbara Tenenbaum, "Why Tita Didn't Marry the Doctor, — or Mexican History in Like Water for Chocolate" in Donald F. Stevens (ed.), *Based on a True Story: Latin American History at the Movies* (Wilmington: Scholarly Resource Books, 1997), p. 171.

[10] Ronald Inglehart. *et al.*, *The North American Trajectory: Cultural, Economic and Political Ties Among the United States, Canada and Mexico* (New York: Aldine de Gruyter, 1996).

co-production, Maria Novaro's *El Jardín del Edén/The Garden of Eden* answered the question of a possible Mexican participation in a North American region rather more ambiguously. Set in the border between Tijuana and San Diego and filmed entirely on location, the film, in a docu-drama style, tells the story of four characters: Serena, a young Mexican widow who has come to the border with her children to live with Juana, an aunt of hers; Felipe, a peasant trying to cross the border illegally to find both work and his family on "the other side;" Liz, a Chicana artist looking for her roots and Jane, an American woman whose brother studies the lives of whales and lives in Mexico. Jane is fascinated by the apparent authenticity of Mexican identity and traditions. What they all have in common however is that they seem to be in search for identity, and national identity is offered as a way to fill the vacuum. As put by a Chicana who is interviewed in one of the scenes, she perceives herself to be "an image" that is "empty" and "what would make that person really full would be being Indian and Mexicana". At the same time, this identity is shown to be contingent: its performative dimension is brought to the foreground in those scenes where Serena's girls are playing, wearing traditional Mexican clothes while teaching Lupita, the Chicana's daughter, the words for them in Spanish, where Felipe is getting dressed in what appears to be a charro suit, along with his rejection of the baseball cap that Jane hands him because it wouldn't match, and in the recreation of the scene depicted in one of Frida Khalo's paintings, namely "Las dos Fridas", which Liz stages with the help of an Indian woman for a video she is making. Thus national identity, which originally seemed to be essential almost in a Romantic fashion, turns out to be a matter of images, attainable only momentarily and only in mirrors, photos and videos; more Baudrillard than Plato in the future for Mexicanidad it seems.

Moreover, the Mexican identity, which in religious decorations, clashing colours and traditional food at times seems to saturate every frame, is also shown to be disturbingly contingent through the narrative. The presence of many Mexicans who despite their nationality cannot speak Spanish, the use of the word "there" that Felipe employs to refer not to the United States but to his hometown in the phrase: "There we have other food, we eat in a different way", and above all the presence of whales which have no nationality although they are in Mexican waters, all work to de-naturalise the taken-for-grantedness of national identity.

So what then of the purported unity between Mexico and the United States sought by neo-liberal elites and preached in their discourses? In this respect, *The Garden of Eden* does seem to imply there is not much difference, at least for most Mexican migrants, between Mexico and the United States. Although shots of a high and modern Bank of America building and a highway are chosen to introduce "the US", the fields where the peasants work are shown to be identical to the Mexican side, inhabited by pretty much the same people who continue living their lives amidst the same traditions. We see the suffering of these Mexican immigrants, but it comes from their compatriots, who mug and beat Felipe, as much as from *la migra*, and at the same time we learn from the news a character is listening to that the Mexican government is also deporting Chinese illegal immigrants. In addition, what we see to stand for "the United States" are some Cadillacs from the 1950s, the motel that gives the film its title, that is, the Garden of Eden, and a walkman. It is hard to make "the American dream" out of these. By comparison, the way indigenous women are presented, sharing in a community spirit even while preparing traditional dishes and shot against the light so as to endow them with a surreal aura, thoroughly romanticises their appearance. Poverty does not seem to be much of a problem. Children still play hide and seek among the piles of second hand clothes their aunt sells for a living, and the poorest of the Indian braceros in the US manage to raise money to send the body of their dead child back to Mexico for burial. Their sombre dignity is beyond pecuniary issues anyway. Moreover, just as Liz, the Chicana character is now so American that she cannot even speak Spanish properly, and there are some 24 million American citizens like her, implying part of the US is already Mexican in some way, Mexicans are shown to play baseball, that all-American sport whose popularity in the country many deplore as a sign of an equivalent Americanisation.

By the end of the film, Serena's son, who had crossed the border with his friend Felipe, decides to return to Mexico and Felipe himself is deported; having helped them to cross the border hidden in the boot of her car. Seduced by the traditional life that she perceives as real, Jane also returns to Mexico and sets out for a journey to Tabasco. In sum, the film ends with no resolution. The walled garden/desert that is the border turns out to be a paradise lost for everyone.

The second Mexican film to comment on migration to the US in the 1990s was made in 1998. With funds raised from the US, Canada, Spain, France and Mexico, and with a global audience also prominently in mind, Alejandro Springall's farcical comedy *Santitos* does show Mexico and the United States to be somehow complementary, part of a larger North American unit. Here, a Mexican woman, also called Esperanza (Hope) like Tita's niece, refuses to believe that her daughter, who was admitted to hospital for a minor operation, has died. As doctors refuse to let her see the body, arguing she passed away from a mysterious but highly contagious illness and the coffin has already been sealed, she believes instead that her daughter has been kidnapped and sold as a child prostitute. Following advice from the image of a saint that appears to her in the kitchen, Esperanza sets out on a journey to find her daughter, leading all the way from her small town in Veracruz to Los Angeles. Her journey turns out to be one of prostitution, since she believes her daughter to be held captive in a brothel and ends up working there herself. Throughout, her faith in religion gives her strength to go on. Eventually, when she reaches LA she does not find her daughter, but falls in love with a Mexican wrestler called Angel. Realising that her search has failed, however, she renounces love and returns to her country, duly choosing the life of a lonely but respectable childless widow over the individual desires of a young woman, as befits conservative Mexican values. Only her lover follows her back to Mexico and persuades her to leave with him again to the US. The film ends with Esperanza tearing down from a wall in her house a mirror in which the ghost of her daughter would sometimes appear and that she then takes with her in a van to the United States.

In sum, the film says yes, there is *esperanza* for Mexicans in the North, and if only they are courageous enough they will be able to bring even their roots along. There is a Mexico beyond its borders, where the experience will not be one of estrangement and exile but as authentic as that grounded on the southern soil. Significantly, and contrary to most films where "Mexico" is always signified as nature in shots of either a desert or a jungle, while "the United States" is invariably the glittering landscape of an urban metropolis, in this film Los Angeles is depicted exactly like Mexico in every respect, populated by mostly Mexican or Mexican American people who all speak Spanish. Although Esperanza's journey to the US is presented as one of prostitution, the take on it is very light indeed, almost like a fairy tale. The "angel" with whom she falls in love successfully fights and defeats his opponent, *la migra* (the border patrol). And what makes Esperanza quit her search in the end is the reflection of a Virgin of Guadalupe on a traffic sign reading "STOP". When she turns around she sees this image comes from a mural where the Virgin is depicted among various flags, and surprised to find her there Esperanza remarks: "You too came all the way down here? The things one does for one's children, doesn't one?"

What then of the Border Cinema, those very low budget films of, as put by Norma Iglesias, extremely "poor technical and narrative quality" but which are nonetheless hugely popular with migrant audiences in both sides of the border, the only places where they are actually shown?[11] Apart from a predictable rise in the number of films made per year, research on representations of the border found that while in the 1980s most plots were about drug dealings and the actual thrills and adventures of crossing, during the 1990s plots revolved instead around an identity crisis, in which "characters confront an encounter between two national cultures".[12] However, no information is yet available on how these films solved the crisis.

To conclude, do these representations match efforts in other discursive realms such as the ones outlined above to construct a different kind of hybridity, namely a cultural hybridity that would act as the ethnic basis of what we might term a post-national state? Judging by the number of films and the conflicting and contradictory representations of Chicanos they put forward, the

---

[11] Norma Iglesias, "Reconstructing the Border: Mexican Border Cinema and its Relationship to its Audience" in Joanna Hershfield and David Maciel (eds), *Mexico's Cinema, a Century of Film and Filmmakers* (Wilmington: Scholarly Resource Books, 1999), p. 235.
[12] Iglesias, "Reconstructing the Border", p. 234.

answer would seem to be no. Moreover, given the lukewarm reception these films received in the box office, it would also seem the narratives did not provide convincing sources of identification for most viewers. Novaro's film was deemed an art-house product but it failed to get any major prizes and *Santitos* grossed little more than $900,000 over its 3 months of exhibition in the US, making it to only 92 screens in total. Rather, it would seem that it was in those films that dealt with the topic tangentially instead of openly that a Mexico formerly viewed as Amenicanised is simply viewed as modern. One such instance would be the yuppie sex comedies like *Sex, Shame and Tears* (Serrano, 1999) and *Cilantro y Perejil* (Montero, 1996), depicting an upper class that appears to be fully Westernised, or the more recent films that sought to undermine the legitimacy of the PRI and its revolutionary nationalism, like *Herod's Law* (Estrada, 2000). In any case, the 1990s seem to have seen the rise and fall of integrationist aspirations. Elsewhere in the continent, the left is on the rise, and it is highly likely that in Mexico itself a PRD government might turn to some sort of revolutionary nationalism again. After all, as Paul Gilroy would put it, tradition, especially with regards to national identity, is often a "changing same".[13]

[13] Paul Gilroy, "Sounds Authentic — Black Music, Ethnicity and the Challenge of a Changing Same", *Journal of Black Music Research* 11, 2 (1991).

Cultural re-Visions, Performance and Display

What (Brazilian) Cultural Studies Can Learn From Tropicália[1]

Robert Stam
New York University

The term "Cultural Studies" is a discursive magnet; its very vagueness makes it a sliding signifier which attracts a wide variety of tendencies. Rather than a reified set of doctrines, Cultural Studies is a constellation of discourses, both a tumult within disciplines and a transdiciplinary umbrella over them. For many of us, it is simply a taken-for-granted part of our research or teaching, but hardly the whole picture.

In Brazil, Cultural Studies is sometimes seen as an "ideia fora de lugar"(an out of place or misplaced idea), just one more trend imposed by the Global North on the Global South, within the unequal global division of intellectual labour. How we see the "misplaced idea" question has everything to do with how we see Cultural Studies itself. It is useful, in this sense, to distinguish between three dimensions of the Cultural Studies project: first, the grids and gurus deployed; second, the corpuses and practices studied; and third, the focus or angle of view. When Cultural Studies is defined in terms of its first dimensions, its grids and gurus, such as Gramsci, Williams, Stuart Hall etc. — the "misplaced" charge is only partially accurate. While it is true that the Anglo-American Academy enjoys an unduly privileged position in the world academic scene, that does not mean that the thinkers themselves are merely local figures artificially made universal. The problem is not that Stuart Hall is known around the world; the problem is that his Latin American counterparts are not.

On the other hand, the very question of gurus does provoke us to ask questions about the genealogy of Cultural Studies itself. The usual account is Anglo-diffusionist: the movement is historicised as beginning in Birmingham and then spreading elsewhere. With all due respect for the invaluable contributions of the Birmingham School,

[1] This paper was first presented at the BRASA (Brazilian Studies Association) Conference at Vanderbilt University in Nashville, in November, 2006.

however, one might easily posit a more diffuse and international para-genealogy, composed of such post-war figures as Roland Barthes and Henri Lefebvre in France, Leslie Fiedler and James Baldwin in the United States, Frantz Fanon, Aime Cesaire and C.R.L. James in the Francophone Afro-diaspora. Or one could go back even earlier to Bakhtin's work in the Soviet Union, and Kracauer in Germany, both in the 1920s and 1930s. One could also call attention to some unsung Brazilian (or quasi-Brazilian) precursors, for example, Antonio Candido, with his distinctive mix of sociology and literary theory, or Roger Bastide, the French anthropologist who spent decades in Brazil, with his transdisciplinary studies of such varied phenonema as candomble, transe, racial prejudice, and literary modernism. One could even point back to the multi-talented Mario de Andrade, who mingled in his art and writing, already in the 1920s, a wide spectrum of disciplines and arts in a splendid rhapsody of analysis and creation.

If we take the second dimension – the corpus studied – the "misplaced" charge is partially accurate. Anglo-American cultural studies is indeed much too monolingual and much too absorbed in contemplating the navel of Anglo-American mass-mediated culture, which is why cultural studies is sometimes derided as "Madonna Studies" or "Star Trek Studies". At its worst, Cultural Studies becomes the academic appendage of the entertainment industry – adept at spotting brief moments of "resistance" — and at its best it becomes a critique of that industry. But whether critical or complicit, Anglo-American cultural studies has often remained ethnocentric in its focus on Anglophone mass-culture. In this sense, North-based cultural studies needs to transnationalise itself by becoming knowledgeable about multiple cultures, and especially those of the Global South, and thus move toward equalising and democratising the too often one-way currents of cultural exchange. Taking the multi-art movement Tropicália, which began in Brazil in the late 1960s, rather than Madonna and Britney Spears, as one's focus, for example, has the effect of decentering a metrocentric field. A study of Tropicália also leads off into the real-world circuitries of cultural policy, necessarily shading off into such contextual issues as censorship under the US-supported dictatorship, Tropicália's vexed relation to the orthodox left, the role of transnational corporations in disseminating popular music, and now, with the prominent exponent of Tropicália, Gilberto Gil as a Brazlilian government minister, into globalisation and intellectual property rights.

It is in relation to the third dimension – focus — often summed up as the "mantra" of class, race, gender, nation, and sexuality – that the charge is least relevant, and this for a simple reason. These axes of identity and social stratification are by definition relevant to all countries, in that they are symptoms of what Bakhtin calls the "heteroglossia" or the many-languagedness of all social formations. Thus one finds, including in Brazil, two distinct critiques of the deployment of the mantra in cultural studies, one, from the left, which argues that cultural studies does not probe these issues in sufficient depth or with sufficient sense of "intersectionality", and another, from the right, that laments the neglect of "literature" in the name of the supposedly crude concerns indexed by the mantra.

My goal here will be to situate "Brazilian Cultural Studies" in relation to other cognate discursive fields by examining the Brazilian multi-art movement called Tropicália. Inaugurated in 1967, the movement was triggered by a cultural explosion in which Glauber Rocha's film *Terra em Transe* (Land in Transe, 1967) Ze Celso's play *Rei da Vela* (King of the Candle), 1967 and Oiticicca's installation "Tropicália" (also 1967)– after which the movement was named — were key catalysing elements. Tropicália became famous especially through two of its key figures – the musicians/composers/writers Gilberto Gil and Caetano Veloso. In this essay, I will correlate Tropicália at its best with Cultural Studies, including Brazilian Cultural Studies. I hasten to add that I am not doing a survey of all the cultural studies work performed – that would be impossible. Nor am I endorsing all the real-life political choices of the Tropicálist artists. Tropicália here serves as a locus of comparison, and as a locus of analysis, in that I will both be seeing Tropicália as a form of culture studies, and be doing cultural studies-style analysis of some Tropicália songs. But the ultimate goal will be to posit Tropicália as a catalyst for what might be called the "transnational turn" in Cultural Studies.

Why Tropicália?

So — why Tropicália? First, the Tropicália "project" itself has always had a Cultural Studies dimension. As intellectuals who write books and dialogue with other intellectuals and who use music to comment on the burning issues of the time, the Tropicálist artists themselves perform cultural theory. Caetano Veloso and Gilberto Gil, in this sense, constitute what might be called "Orphic Intellectuals", or, playing on Antonio Gramsci, "Orpheoganic intellectual". They are not only the creators of popular culture; they are also its theoreticians. In a multi-media intervention, they enact the cultural studies debates in visual, sensuous, written, lyrical, percussive, and with Gilberto Gil as Minister in the Lula Government, even in policy form.[2]

Second, the relation between cultural studies and more established disciplines is in some ways analogous to the relation between Tropicália and more established genres of music. Just as Tropicália is not a genre of music *per se*, but rather a meta-commentary on the relationship between various genres of music, so Cultural Studies is not an academic discipline but rather a transdisciplinary ferment active within and between many disciplines.

Third, both Cultural Studies and Tropicália treat popular culture as a valid form of artistic and political expression, and thus undermine the conventional low art/high art hierarchy. Both movements are anti-canonical, disrespectful of consecrated genres. Much as Dick Hebdige valorised punk and mod and reggae[3] so Tropicália has valorised cultural manifestations which a certain elite found peripheral, tacky, déclassé, or brega (tacky). For both movements, the socially marginalised, to pick up on an expression that Stuart Hall borrowed from Stallybrass and White, could be seen as "symbolically central".

Fourth, as a kind of Cultural studies avant-la-lettre, Tropicália has granted itself the right to speak about anything and everything. The Tropicálists are certainly not the only pop musicians to speak

---

[2] In terms of policy, Gil has fostered the decentralisation of film production (away from Rio de Janeiro and Sao Paulo toward the Northeast, for example), promoted Brazilian HipHop, and raised issues of "intellectual copyright" in favour of taking some control away from multinational corporations.

[3] Dick Hebdige, *Subculture: The Meaning of Style* (London: Routledge, 1979).

of the cinema in their lyrics, for example, but they are probably the only ones to offer a critical history of a film movement in a song ("Cinema Novo" from *Tropicália II*). And what other pop musicians actually dialogue with literary intellectuals in their work? When literary critic/theorist Roberto Schwarz wrote that Tropicália held Brazilian contradictions "up to the white light of ultra-modernity, thus revealing its absurdity", Caetano answered in a song lyric, using a pun. Brazil may be "absurdo (absurd)", he said, "but it is not surdo" – the reference is both to the word for "deaf" and to the big bass-drum that orients the samba pageant – since it "has a musical ear".

Fifth, Tropicália and Cultural Studies share a critically distanced stance toward antecedent left cultural theory – notably toward Frankfurt School-style Adornonian pessimism about popular culture in the case of Cultural Studies, and toward national leftist aesthetic anti-imperialism in the case of Tropicália. The Frankfurt School and the media-imperialism school both had in common, after all, the idea that the couch-potato consumers of mass-culture, whether in the pampered North or the oppressed Global South, exercised little agency or resistance.

Art, we know, is sometimes precocious, existing "in advance" of academic theorisation. Tropicália, in this sense, shares certain social themes with Cultural Studies. The cultural studies movement, especially in its postcolonial variant, has favoured a whole series of tropes of mixing: syncretism, hybridity, creolisation, miscegenation and so forth. Gil's song "From Bob Dylan to Bob Marley: A Provocation Samba" in this sense, traces the origins of hybridity in what might be called the colonial rape as the dark side of modernity. "When Bob Dylan converted to Christianity", the song begins, "he made a reggae album as a form of compensation. Abandoning the people of Israel, he rediscovered Judaism while going back the wrong way". The song thus traces the "roots" and "routes" of Afro-diasporic culture, ranging over five centuries and diverse continents, creatively counter-pointing the early 16th century — "when Africans arrived in Brazil" and the late 20th century – the era of Bob Dylan, Bob Marley and Michael Jackson. Syncretism, for Gil, is power-laden; rooted not only in multicultural celebration but also in the fraught contact zones of colonial power. When "Africans adopted Our Lord of Bomfim", the lyrics suggest, it was an act "both of resistance and surrender". The final refrain indexes two forms of syncretism, one liberating and the other alienated, personified respectively by Bob Marley and Michael Jackson: The refrain: "Bob Marley died/Because besides being black/He was Jewish/ Michael Jackson/ meanwhile/ is still around, but besides becoming white/ he's become very sad".

Another shared feature of Cultural Studies and Tropicália relates to its articulations of race and class; the Caetano song "Haiti" in this sense, gives musical flesh to Stuart Hall's famous formulation that "race is the modality in which class is lived". To my mind, "Haiti" addresses racial and class oppression in the Black Atlantic in ways that complement and even transcend the methods of social science and does it in a way that directly impacts both the mind and the senses.

The song was inspired by an episode that Caetano actually witnessed. As he was about to receive a "Citizenship Award", he observed a demonstration of the lack of citizenship in Brazil, as a multi-racial group of cops beat up a multi-racial group of ordinary Bahians. The "scene" of the song is the roof of the Jorge Amado Foundation in Salvador, named after the world-famous Bahian novelist lauded by some critics as the bard of racial democracy, and by others as the folkloric exoticiser of blacks. The narration is focalised by those invited to a party, where they witness the following scene:

> …soldiers, almost all black/ beat up black malandros
> beat up mulatto thieves and other thieves, almost white
> but treated like blacks/ just to show to the others, almost black
> and they are almost all black
> and to the almost white, but poor like blacks
> how it is that blacks, poor people, and mulattoes
> and almost white, almost black from being so poor
> how it is that they are to be treated.
> And it doesn't matter if the eyes of the entire world
> Might alight for a moment on the square
> Where slaves were punished

Thus the lyrics link the legacy of slavery and the pillory – i.e. the popular tourist attraction called "Pelourinho" (literally pillory) – as the site of disciplinary punishments – to the present-realities of colour-coded police brutality. At the same time, the composer/ authors hear the sounds of rebellion in the drumming of the Afro—blocos, where uniformed young children learn percussion in an Afro-centric context. Both the lyrics and the percussion in the song invoke Olodum-style drumming:

> And where today a batuque, a batuque
> With the purity of uniformed boys from junior high on parade
>   day
> And the epic grandeur of a people in formation
> Attracts us, dazzles us, and stimulates us.

But this kind of culturalist strength, the song suggests, is ultimately insufficient in a Brazil where citizenship is so fragile and compromised:

> But it doesn't matter
> Not even the trace of the tenement
> Or the Globo TV Show "Fantastic Lens"
> Or the record by Paul Simon
> No one, no one is a citizen.

The refrain, then, alludes to the recombinant, differential commonalities of the Black Atlantic, where Brazil both is like, and is not like, Haiti:

> And if you go to the party in Pelourinho
> And even if you don't think about Haiti
> Pray for Haiti
> Haiti is here. Haiti isn't here.

The song's refrain — "Haiti is here, Haiti is not here" — alludes to a famous 1881 quotation from the racist philosopher Silvio Romero. Still frightened by the Haitian revolution, Romero said that "Brazil is not, and should not be, Haiti". But here style is inseparable from substance. The song is declaimed in rap style, a style which while it became famous in North America was also intimately linked to Afro-Brazilian currents such as "repente" and "talking sambas". The lyrics link Brazil to other Black Atlantic countries, and specifically to Haiti as site both of the first black revolutionary Republic in the past, and of neo-colonial oppression in the present.

The remainder of the song excoriates reactionary politicians more interested in denouncing abortion than in producing a coherent and democratic educational plan. The song evokes, finally, the historical memory of the "massacre of 111 defenseless prisoners" in Carandiru prison, where "prisoners are almost always black/or almost black, or almost white/ almost black from being so poor". Instead of cordiality, we find the politicisation of avant-gardist dissonance; in sum, the song addresses the latter-day legacies of slavery, both in the negative form of dispossession and brutality, and in the positive form of artistic expression as a sublimation of historical pain.

Sixth, Tropicália, like cultural studies, discerns and actively nourishes a potentially subversive and even utopian element within popular culture. Partly as a reaction against Frankfurt School pessimism, it sees progressive potentialities even within mass culture. Caetano and Gil, in this sense, use music to transfigure historical relationalities in ways at once cosmopolitan, international and very Brazilian. They display a chameleonic ability to move easily between various cultural repertoires, to negotiate multiple worlds in a ludic dance of identities reminiscent of carnival and candomble. Their art is literally utopian – etymologically "no-place" – in terms of its mobile, planetary sense of location. Tropicália inhabits, to borrow Caetano's own words about Jorge Bem, "the transhistorical utopian country which we have a duty to construct and which lives inside all of us". Music, in this sense, is not a mere mirror of identity; rather, it shapes, critiques, and fashions new forms of identity and identification. Brazilian music at its best recreates what might be called the utopia of a popular rather than an elitist avant-garde. It creates new registers of feeling, channeling empathy and demonstrating popular art's capacity to give pleasurable, kinetic shape to social desire, to mobilise feeling in a popular and mass-mediated form.

We see this utopian tendency in the music video of Gil's song "Funk-se Quem Puder" (Funk Yourself if You Can) Here are some of the lyrics:

> Funk-Yourself if you can
> It's imperative to dance
> Feel the impulse
> Throw your butt around
> Tasting the Rhythm
> Funk-yourself if you can.
> It's imperative to play
> Fire in the vertebrae.
> Fire in the muscles.
> Music in all the atoms
> Our Atlantic, Athletic, romantic, poetic Republic of Music…
> Funk Youself if you can
> It's time to throw everything upside down
> without panic
> a quick form of playing
> time to swim back to mother Africa
> Africa…Musica… Africa… Musica…

The video shows Gil performing in a neighbourhood – Greenwich Village in New York – which had historically been both Dutch, Afro-Brazilian, and English. The fact is that New York (then New Amsterdam) was connected to Africa and Brazil via the Dutch, that words like "negro" and "pickanninny" (from "pequininho") came into English via Portuguese, that a Black Portuguese pilot named Estevam Gomes navigated the Hudson just one year after Verazzano, and that Brazilised and Americanised Africans with names like Paulo d'Angola (Paul from Angola) and Antonio Portugues (Anthony the Portuguese) were freed and granted their own farms during Dutch rule. Indeed, "SOB's", the Sounds-of-Brazil Nightclub, where Caetano and Gil have often played, stands on land once farmed by an Angolan-Brazilian-American free black named Simao Congo). The music video moves in the end from present-day New York to Sao Paulo, where Gil leads street-kids in a performance of music and break-dance. The visuals of the song break with the slickness of much of music-video by including the city's literally funky street kids, whose costumes and dance moves betray clear familiarity with the Diana Ross/Michael Jackson vehicle *The Wiz* (1978).

The other example of critical utopianism comes from the music video of the Gil song "Mao de Limpeza" (Hand of Cleanliness), performed in the video with Chico Buarque de Holanda. The song's lyrics satirically upend a racist Brazilian proverb that suggests that "blacks, if they don't make a mess at the entrance, will make it at the exit". Calling that view "a damned lie", the singers proceed to undo the association between blackness and dirtiness, linking it instead to the history of white oppression. Both during and after slavery, the song suggests, it was blacks who cleaned up the mess that whites made, and "black", therefore, "is the hand of cleanliness" and "immaculate purity". Here are the lyrics:

> They say that when blacks don't make a mess at the entrance
> They make it at the exit
> Just Imagine!
> The slave mother spent her life
> Cleaning up the mess that whites made
> Just Imagine!/What a damned lie!
> Even after slavery was abolished
> Black continued cleaning clothes/And scrubbing floors
> How the blacks worked and suffered!
> Just Imagine!/Black is the hand of cleanliness
> Of life consumed at the side of the stove
> Black is the hand that puts food on the table
> And cleans with soap and water
> Black is the hand of Immaculate Purity
> They say when blacks don't make a mess at the entrance
> They make it at the exit
> What a damned lie!
> Look at the dirty white guy!

The visuals of the video further complicate the meaning of the song. The phenotypically white singer Chico appears in blackface, while Gil, the black, appears in whiteface. The reference is double, both to the "boneca de pixe" (tar baby) tradition (from both Brazil and the United States) and to the racist American tradition of minstrelcy. In the US, the issues of blackface and minstrelcy are very fraught. The Spike Lee film *Bamboozled* (2000) satirically invoked minstrelcy, thus winning praise but also making people nervous. Ted Danson and Whoopi Goldberg played with the conventions of minstrelcy, but got severely "burned" in the process. In Brazil, the black community vigorously protested the casting of a white actor in blackface in a 1968 version of "Uncle Tom's Cabin". But "Hand of Cleanliness" is written and performed in a completely different spirit. Here, the idea for using blackface comes not from white media entrepreneurs but from the black artist. In a sly Brazilian version of the costumed racial inversions of Genet's *Les Noirs* (1958), the song overturns the racist binarism which equates whiteness with cleanliness and blackness with dirtiness; here blackness connotes immaculate purity, while whiteness connotes the dirtiness of the branco sujao. "Hand of Cleanliness" provokes a Brechtian alienation effect, estranging the doxa of racist common sense. Imagine! How could anyone ever have associated blackness with dirtiness! Even the style is Brechtian in that it recuperates an "incorrect" stereotype within an anti-illusionistic aesthetic. In minstrelcy, blackface was unilateral; there was no whiteface. Blackface was premised on whiteness as normative and blackness as intrinsically comic and grotesque. But here the idea of blackface comes not from white media entrepreneurs but from the black artist himself. At the same time, the parodic and stylised performance itself implies the transcendence of the black/white binarism: the two singers are obviously friends, obviously playing at carnival, and obviously having a very good time. The racism of the proverb does not mean that whites and blacks cannot be friends or fight together against racism.

The uses and abuses of comparison

The Tropicálists practice cultural comparison not only in their writings and interviews but also in their songs. Caetano's "Os Americanos" (The Americans, 1987) for example, suggests that "For Americans, white is white, and black is black/and the mulata is not the greatest/Gays are gays, machos are machos/ Women are women and money is money/ while in the South indefinition reigns."[4]

---

[4] Present author's translation.

We non-Brazilians who do "Brazilian Studies" are also, in a way, comparatists. Part of our fascination with Brazil has to do with the analogies and disanalogies between the histories and cultures of our own country and those of Brazil. In terms of the comparison with the US, it is a matter of two multiracial countries marked by conquest, colonialism, slavery, and immigration. In the Brazilian case, it is a matter not only of these historical comparabilities but also of the vast interext of US/Brazil comparisons as the inevitable backdrop of discussions of national identity. Brazil and the United States, in sum, are deeply enmeshed in a specular, mirror-like play of sameness and difference, identity and alterity, affection and suspicion. While in no way identical, the two countries are eminently comparable. The same elements exist, but reshuffled. What is a major chord in one country becomes a minor chord in the other.

Many of the Brazilian theorists of national identity, in Brazil — for example, Paulo Prado, Gilberto Freyre, Sergio Buarque de Holanda, Raimundo Faoro, Vianna Moog, Roberto da Matta and countless others — have implicitly or explicitly invoked the US-Brazil comparison. These comparisons are asymmetrical and power-laden, of course, since Brazilians make the comparison from a position of relative geo-political weakness, although they also make it, in the Bush-era from a position of infinitely greater popularity in the world, at a time when the US is roundly detested in much of the world. Yet in historical terms, metaphors of Brazil and the US as "twins" or "sisters" or "cousins" have proliferated over the centuries. But the familial tropes can not completely hide the fact that these "kinship relations" were always necessarily haunted by inequality.

Cross-national comparisons can serve myriad purposes. They can move along a spectrum that goes from a maximalist and demonising differentialism – "we have nothing in common with them!" — to a paternalistic "Good Neighbour" camaraderie – "we have everything in common (but don't forget that you're subordinate!") – to a more nuanced approach which stresses the differentiated commonalities within asymmetrical power relations.

At its best, comparison becomes not an exercise in national narcissism but rather a cognitive instrument for exploring the analogies and disanalogies between various national formations.

What (Brazilian) Cultural Studies Can Learn From Tropicália

Here Caetano provides an example in his alertness both to very real differences between Brazil and the US and to a common cultural substratum. One of the most remarkable passages in Caetano's memoir *Tropical Truth* is the one where Caetano expresses his surprise at feeling instantly at ease in New York City, more even than in Portugal, because he knew that he was, as in Bahia or Sao Paulo, "in the Americas".[5] Unlike those who draw simplistic contrasts between a supposedly mestizo Brazil and a white US. Caetono sees the US, "no less than Brazil but differently, and despite an official desire not to recognize the fact", as "inevitably mestizo, inevitably marked by the non-whites which colonisation decimated and enslaved". Despite official denials, what Caetano calls a "deep miscegenation" has taken place in both countries.

Since mononational forms of cultural studies can become ethnocentric, and since bilateral comparison runs the risk of dualism, Brazilian cultural studies should strive to be polynational and multi-perspectival. Tropicália, in this sense, anticipated a recent tendency, on the part of many disciplines and intellectual movments to move beyond the nation state as a unit of analysis. The emphasis on the "Black Atlantic" rather on individual nation states, forms part of this dynamic. The transnational move is reflected as well in the popularity of such words as "global", "diasporic", "transcultural", "exilic", "transational" and so forth. The frequency of aquatic metaphors – Paul Gilroy's "Black Atlantic", Kamau Brathwaite's "Tidelectics" (instead of Dialectics), Joe Roach's "circum-Atlantic performance", J. Lorand Matory's "circum-oceanic" and so forth – is also a symptom of this same transnationalising process. It is not a question simply of "comparing" cultures — of placing distinct and separate histories side by side, as it were — but rather of counterpointing cultures, seeing both the glaring differences and the common currents flowing through them, the ways their histories interpenetrate and interact.

Tropicália, in this sense, boldly interweaves global references on both a musical and lyrical/verbal level. Rather than address Brazil alone, Tropicália takes the entire world as its province. It reflects, and reflects on, Brazil's structural, affective, and artistic openness to Europe, Africa, North America, and the indigenous world, indeed

[5] Caetano Veloso, *Tropical Truth: A Story of Music and Revolution in Brazil* (New York: DaCapo, 2002).

to the entire globe. Caetano's CD, *Noites do Norte* (2003), for example, provides an exemplary instance of this process. As a kind of "Black Atlantic" CD, *Noites do Norte* moves from Nigeria and "Two Naira fifty Kobo" and the Angola of "Congo Benguela Manjolo Cabinda Mina" to the auctions of slavery to "Zumbi" and Joaquim Nabuco on to "Treize de Maio". In short, the CD reaches back in time and outward in space, composing, in the end, a veritable musical essay on the history of the Afro-diaspora. Gilberto Gil, for his part, is a veritable bard of the Black Atlantic. Not only has he performed with musicians like Jimmy Cliff, Stevie Wonder, and Youssou N'Dour, he has also referred both lyrically and stylistically to the variegated musical forms of the Black Atlantic.

It is well-known that Tropicália saw itself as a "new dentition" of 1920s Brazilian modernism, with its key trope of artistic "anthropophagy". While the modernists devoured dada and surrealism, the Tropicálists devoured Jimi Hendrix and the Beatles. The original formulations of modernist cannibalism had a negative and positive pole. The negative pole had to do with the critique of the cannibalist social Darwinism of bourgeois capitalist society, while the positive pole had to do with the valorisation of aboriginal matriarchy and communal egalitarianism as a utopian model for a society free of coercion.

The problem with modernist discourse about the Indian was its metaphorical, allegorical character, in that the movement never linked its ideas with the struggles of the actually existing Indians of Brazil. In this sense, modernism prolonged 19th century Romanticism's exaltation of a safely remote and symbolic Indian, without actually engaging with the flesh-and-blood Indians being dispossessed around Brazil. With the advent, beginning in the 1980s, of "indigenous media", we find the present-day avatars of Oswald's "indio tecnizado" or "high-tech Indian". The practitioners of "indigenous media" use the new media technologies to preserve and reinvigorate their traditions, protect their land, and strategise against dispossession and cultural alienation; the media become a recombinant means of communal invention, a form of technological anthropophagy.

It is interesting to reflect, in this context, on Gilberto Gil's recent interventions, in his role of Minister of Culture, in the debates about "intellectual property rights". Gil has frequently defended the idea of "open source software". In the spirit of indigenous notions of communal property, Gil also tried to release some of his songs under the Creative Commons License, so that others could freely "cannibalise" them. In this sense, Gil tries to enact in policy the positive pole of the cannibal metaphor, to wit, the social desirability of indigenous communal culture and its refusal of private property and class inequality. In a generous gesture of digital cannibalism and recombinant transtextuality, Gil, who has himself devoured so many influences, thus offered the body of his own work to be devoured by others.

Conclusion

Like Modernism in the 1920s, Tropicália in the 1960s absorbed and transformed antecedent forms and genres while trying to reverse the unequal currents of global cultural exchange. Tropicália, like Modernism, worked from a basis of an artistic self-confidence that taunted and outwitted the geo-political powers that be. In a similar way, Brazilian Cultural Studies, as a relatively marginalised field both within Cultural Studies and within Area Studies, can learn from Tropicália. Hardly an island, Brazilian culture studies is connected both to many established disciplines and to many emerging discursive formations, including: diaspora studies, comparative race studies, subaltern studies, cultural policy studies, urban studies, Black Atlantic Studies, multicultural studies, indigenous studies, critical race theory, radical pedagogy, whiteness studies, postcolonial studies, transnational feminist studies, Francophone studies, minor transnational studies, globalisation studies, counter-globalisation studies, and what Walter Mignolo and others have called the "Coloniality/Modernity Project".[6] What all these fields, or at least their more radical wings, have in common is their leveling thrust, their critique of Eurotropic hierarchies, and their nuanced engagement with the "mantra" or nation, race, gender, and sexuality.

Interesting things happens when we add Brazil into these preexisting intellectual formations. The Black Atlantic alters its

[6] See Walter D. Mignolo, *The Idea of Latin America* (Oxford: Blackwell, 2005).

shape when Brazil is included. Native American Studies becomes transformed when native Brazil is incorporated. The work on diasporic black intellectuals (for example, that by Brent Hayes Edwards) gains texture when one factors in the work of Abdias de Nascimento and the journal *Quilombo*. Our job as practitioners of Brazilian cultural studies is to demonstrate that Brazil is not an "add on"; rather, it can actually change pre-existing disciplines and discursive formations.

Like Tropicália songs, Brazilian Cultural Studies can forge mutually haunting connections between worlds and histories, and between widely divergent yet linked times and spaces and nations. We can take advantage of the cognitive power of transnational comparison and the "mutual illumination" it affords, emphasising what is gained in approaching these issues in a transnational manner. Rather than segregate historical periods and geographical regions into neatly fenced off areas of expertise, we can assert their interconnectedness, within a permeable interwoven relationality, particularly in a transnational age typified by the global "travel" of images, sounds, goods and populations.

On Late Imperial Culture:
the Case of the Habsburg Monarchy

Jonathan Kwan
University of Nottingham

In his final book – assembled posthumously from essays and lectures into a coherent work – Edward Said meditates on "late style", a term he adopts from Adorno's fragmentary observations on Beethoven's late works. Said's first chapter is taken from a lecture on bodily condition and aesthetic style given nine years after his diagnosis with leukaemia:

> The body, its health, its care, composition, functioning, and flourishing, its illnesses and demise, belong to the order of nature; what we *understand* of that nature, however, how we see and live it in our consciousness, how we create a sense of our life individually and collectively, subjectively as well as socially, how we divide it into periods, belongs roughly speaking to the order of history that when we reflect on it we can recall, analyse, and meditate on, constantly changing its shape in process.[1]

In effect, Said is asking fundamental questions about "timeliness". Are there appropriate stages to life and history? Is there a natural development – beginning, growth, maturity, decline and death – not just for human life but also for societies, aesthetic fashions, states and empires? Indeed, is all human thought and action subject to an overarching natural framework? Aristotle had postulated such an organic frame of understanding in his *Physics* and Said applies this concept to modern culture and history. Here Said's touchstone, as in so many of his other works, is Theodor Adorno; like Said a wide-ranging, all-encompassing intellectual who investigated the links between politics, society and culture. For Adorno, late Beethoven, above all the final quartets are "not well rounded, but wrinkled, even fissured".[2] In monumental acts

[1] Edward Said, *On Late Style* (London: Bloomsbury, 2006), p. 3.
[2] Theodor Adorno, *Beethoven: The Philosophy of Music* (Cambridge: Polity

of defiance, Beethoven's late works "cast off the illusion of art ... [and] leave only fragments behind".[3] These are not late works produced in an autumnal glow of hard-won wisdom, of indulgence and serenity.

> [Beethoven] does not bring about their harmonious synthesis. As a dissociative force he tears them apart in time, perhaps in order to preserve them for the eternal. In the history of art, late works are catastrophes.[4]

This essay will apply Said's and Adorno's ideas on "lateness" and "timeliness" to the specific context of Vienna at the turn-of-the-century. Despite the wealth of scholarship in the wake of Schorske's groundbreaking book on Viennese politics and culture published in 1981, little consideration has been paid to the concept of "lateness".[5] There has been no sustained attempt to place the Habsburg Monarchy within the traditional paradigm characterising the rise and fall of Empire.[6] Part of this neglect is no doubt the suspicion of grand narratives in the tradition of Gibbon, Toynbee, Spengler and, recently, Paul Kennedy. Nevertheless, such common terms as "late Habsburg Monarchy" and "late Imperial Vienna" implicitly invoke a standard life cycle of empires.[7] Is this simply a

---

Press, 1998), p. 123.

[3] Adorno, *Beethoven*, p. 125.

[4] Adorno, *Beethoven*, p. 126.

[5] Carl Schorske, *Fin-de-Siècle Vienna: Politics and Culture* (New York: Vintage Books, 1981).

[6] Despite grand title of Alan Sked, *The Decline and Fall of the Habsburg Monarchy* (London: Longman, 1989) his book is in fact a well-argued long historiographical essay. In English perhaps C.A. Macartney, *The Habsburg Empire 1790-1918* (London: Weidenfeld and Nicolson, 1968) has the scale and ambition but there is no comparative aspect and his interpretation is hardly made explicit throughout the book. In German, Hugo Hantsch, *Die Geschichte Österreichs1648-1918* (Graz: Styria, 1953) and Erich Zöllner, *Geschichte Österreichs. Von Anfang bis zur Gegenwart* (Vienna: Verlag für Geschichte und Politik, 1966) attempt to describe Austria's rise and fall but there is little desire to draw general conclusions or create some sort of topology.

[7] For example T. Mills Kelly, "Political Trials in the Late Habsburg Monarchy", *Nationalities Papers* 27, 2 (1999), pp. 175-89 and John Boyer,

retrospective use of "late" in the knowledge that the Monarchy would fall apart in 1918 or is there a sense or consciousness of "lateness" in Vienna's rich culture at the turn-of-the-century? In sum, how useful are Said's and Adorno's concepts to understanding the culture and society of Vienna 1900?

Said in his book only mentions Vienna in passing, yet there are many threads which point to Vienna as a primary location of "late style". Beethoven, Richard Strauss, Arnold Schoenberg – all treated in depth by Said – were closely connected to Viennese musical life. Adorno, in his early twenties, spent two crucial years of study in Vienna. Hermann Broch in his brilliant dissection of Vienna described it as "museumish" (das Museale), a "gay apocalypse".[8]

This essay is divided into two sections; the first will attempt to uncover concepts of "lateness" within the cultural world of Vienna 1900 while the second focuses on the most Viennese of operas *Der Rosenkavalier* (1909), applying Said's concept of the "return to the eighteenth century". Where Said concentrates on Richard Strauss and the "massive and recurring presence of the eighteenth century in his work", I will incorporate Strauss's collaborator, the precocious poet and Viennese aesthete, Hugo von Hofsmannsthal, into the discussion. Not only was he the source of Rosenkavalier's setting and basic story, but his literary production contains constant references to the eighteenth century, particularly to Venice and its errant son, Casanova.

H. Stuart Hughes has eloquently characterised the mood in early twentieth century Europe:

[I]n the generation just preceding the First World War these thinkers similarly shared a wider experience of psychological *malaise*: the sense of impending doom, of old practices and institutions no longer conforming to social realities ...[9]

Political Radicalism in Late Imperial Vienna: Origins of the Christian Social Movement, 1848-1897 (Chicago: Chicago University Press, 1981).

[8] Hermann Broch, "Hugo von Hofmannsthal and his Time: Art and its Non-Style at the End of the Nineteenth Century" in Hermann Broch, *Geist and Zeitgeist. The Spirit in an Unspiritual Age* (1947-8; New York: Counterpoint, 2002), p. 178-81.

[9] H. Stuart Hughes, *Conscious and Society* (1958; New Brunswick:

Yet Hughes, as many other scholars, does not investigate the exact contours of this ominous atmosphere. Above all, in the language of fin-de-siècle Europe, there were two words in common use which indicated a consciousness of decline, of ill health within the body politic and modern society in general – degeneration and decadence. While there is some overlap between the terms, *degeneration* tapped into the discourse of medical science and the Darwinian theory of evolution, while *decadence* implied a general moral, spiritual, cultural and intellectual decline not necessarily linked to any scientific or biological explanations.

The second half of the nineteenth century witnessed an outpouring of books on social evolution, degeneration, morbidity and perversion – all claiming a medical, biological or physical anthropological basis.[10] Why was this the case? Daniel Pick cites the "apparent paradox that civilisation, science, and economic progress might be the catalyst if, as much as the defence against, physical and social pathology".[11] In other words, progress may in turn produce political, societal, psychological and physiological degeneration. One of the most prominent voices in the debate was Max Nordau, who grew up in the German-speaking Budapest Jewish community but spent most of his life practising medicine and writing books and journalism in Paris. Nordau's most famous book *Degeneration* (1892-3) mixed a working knowledge of the scientific literature with a journalist's skill in synthesis, vivid language and dramatic images. His claims were far reaching: "[w]e stand now in the midst of a severe mental epidemic; of a sort of black death of degeneration and hysteria".[12] Linking material progress with degeneration, Nordau postulated a disturbing disconnect between the speed, innovation and relentless pressure of modern society and the natural rhythms of mankind's biology. Advanced civilisation fatigued and exhausted humanity, inducing hysteria and cultural malaise. He was particularly harsh on contemporary culture criticising its loose morals, cult of mysticism

---

Transaction, 2005), p. 14.

[10] For a representative list of studies see Daniel Pick, *Faces of Degeneration. A European Disorder, c. 1848-c.1918* (Cambridge: Cambridge University Press, 1989), p. 20.

[11] Pick, *Faces of Degeneration,* p. 11.

[12] Quoted in Pick, *Faces of Degeneration,* p. 24.

and pseudo-scientific approach.[13]

Nordau's work was not firmly grounded in any particular local or national tradition. He felt a part of the European-wide intelligentsia concerned with the effects of modernity. Daniel Pick's book *Faces of Degeneration* outlines the different forms and traditions this concern took in France, Italy and England but makes only cursory references to Germany and Austria. What then characterised Viennese discourse on modernity and contemporary mankind? Above all, there was an intense interest in sexuality, in gender and in the internal psychological workings of the mind. Three thinkers stand out: Richard Krafft-Ebing, Otto Weininger and Sigmund Freud. In 1886 Krafft- Ebing, originally from Mannheim but active in Graz and then Vienna for thirty years, published his *Psychopathia Sexualis*, a catalogue of sexual deviancy. Krafft-Ebing's work was both part of a growing preoccupation with sex and an obsession with naming and fixing pathological disorders.[14] In his study entitled *Nervosität und neurathenische Zustände* (1895), Krafft-Ebing echoed the general sentiment that modern life was conducive to nervous disorders:

> The last few decades have seen great changes in the political and social conditions of civilised nations, especially in their mercantile, industrial and agrarian conditions. These changes have substantially affected professional life, one's status as a citizen, and one's possessions – and all at the expense of the nervous system which has to contend with increased social and economic demands through a greater expenditure of energy, often with insufficient relaxation.[15]

The sense of nervous ill-ease is evident in the tortured

---

[13] See Pick, *Faces of Degeneration,* pp. 23-7, P. M. Baldwin, "Liberalism, Nationalism and Degeneration: The Case of Max Nordau", *Central European History* 13, 2 (1980), pp. 99-120, and William Johnstone, *The Austrian Mind. An Intellectual and Social History 1848-1938* (Berkeley: University of California Press, 1972), pp. 362-4.

[14] See Johnstone, *The Austrian Mind,* pp. 229-37.

[15] Quoted in Sigmund Freud, "'Civilized' Sexual Morality and Modern Nervous Illness" in Sigmund Freud, *Civilization and its Discontents* (1908; London: Penguin, 2002), p. 88.

outpourings of Otto Weininger, who attempted to interpret the world through the dialectic of masculinity and femininity, extolling the former and denigrating the latter. *Sex and Character* is a diatribe against women and Jews but at the same time a "serious, comprehensive and emotionally charged ideological critique of modernity in general".[16] The spirit of modernity, he asserts, is dominated by femininity and Jewishness, thus leading to the present condition of cultural degeneration. Shortly after publication of the book, Weininger, at the tender age of 23, melodramatically committed suicide in the house where Beethoven died.

The various strands collect in the most capacious medical and scientific mind in Vienna at the time, Sigmund Freud. He had personal connections with Nordau, Krafft-Ebing and Weininger. The young Freud met Nordau in Paris in 1886, but was unimpressed and did not pursue the acquaintance. In fact, by the 1890s Freud was already questioning the whole concept of degeneration.[17] Freud's encounter with Krafft-Ebing was of a different nature: between an industrious, eager researcher and a distinguished Professor. In April 1896 Freud presented a paper at a local scientific society – Krafft-Ebing was the President – which put forward the novel notion that hysteria was caused by childhood sexual abuse. Freud's theory met with an icy reception and Krafft-Ebing cryptically commented that "it sounds like a scientific fairy tale".[18] A few years later, however, Krafft-Ebing did support Freud's application for a full professorship at the University of Vienna.[19] Finally, with respect to Weininger, it is highly probable that Freud, through a mutual friend, was the indirect source of Weininger's theory of bisexuality.[20] Weininger later visited Freud with the manuscript and a request for a

---

[16] Chandak Sengoopta, *Otto Weininger. Sex, Science, and Self in Imperial Vienna* (Chicago: Chicago University Press, 2000), p. 1. See also Johnstone, *The Austrian Mind*, pp. 158-62.

[17] Pick, *Faces of Degeneration*, p. 101.

[18] For a description of the event see Peter Gay, *Freud. A Life for Our Time* (1988; London: Little Books, 2006), pp. 93-6.

[19] For a full account of Freud's famous battle for a professorship see Gay, *Freud*, pp. 136-41.

[20] See Sengoopta, *Otto Weininger*, p. 15 and Gay, *Freud*, p. 154-6.

recommendation letter. Freud advised against publication and was of the view that the book required ten more years of empirical work.

Freud's view of modern civilisation is in accordance with his theory of psychoanalysis. Thus, in a paper from 1908 entitled "Civilised" Sexual Morality and Modern Nervous Illness, he stressed the "harmful suppression of sexual life in civilised peoples".[21] Thus Freud focuses the attention on sexual drives and their suppression by civilised morality, rather than, as Krafft-Ebing does, on the nervous system. For Freud, each step in civilisation is accompanied by a progressive renunciation of our sex drives.[22] Rather than emphasising the effects of modern life, Freud searches for universal principles: the progressive repression of sexual drives and mankind's innate desire for sexual pleasure. While he disagreed with contemporaries over the causes of modern nervous illness, Freud did not question its increasing prevalence.

Many of these preoccupations are evident in the discourse on *decadence* as a cultural movement. Hermann Bahr, the influential organiser of and writer on Viennese modernism, looked at this new phenomenon in an essay published in 1891.[23] Decadence – which Bahr contrasted to the preceding literary trend, naturalism – contained four characteristics. First, and most importantly, the new decadent writers explored the interior world; a vague, obscure realm of shifting moods and feeling. Bahr called contemporary writers "romantics of the nerves" since they searched for the person's inner nervous temperament. The second aspect was the turn away from nature towards the emotions and actions of man. The third aspect was a search for the mystical, a trend also highlighted in Nordau's book. Finally, Bahr wrote on the use of the exceptional, the extraordinary, even the monstrous to convey the totality of life, especially its dream-like aspects. In other words, to use Hermann Broch's phrase, there was a "breakthrough into the irrational".[24]

---

[21] Freud, *Civilization and its Discontents*, p. 88.

[22] Freud, *Civilization and its Discontents*, p. 90.

[23] Hermann Bahr, "Decadence" in Gotthart Wunberg (ed.), *Wiener Moderne. Literatur, Kunst und Musik zwischen 1890 und 1910* (Stuttgart: Philipp Reclam, 1981), pp. 225-32.

[24] Broch, *Geist and Zeitgeist*, p. 161.

Bahr and his contemporaries pointed to the writer Hugo von Hofmannsthal as exemplifying this trend. Appearing suddenly on the Viennese scene of the early 1890s as a preternaturally mature sixteen year old poet, Hofmannsthal's lyrical poetry stunned the Viennese literary community with its virtuosity, freshness and beauty. Bahr proclaimed Hofmannsthal "a Goethe still sitting on the school bench".[25] Almost inevitably the years from 1899 to 1906 were a transition period for Hofmannsthal, when he matured from prodigy to young man mirrored by his move from poetry to drama (and prose). The most revealing document from this crucial period is the famous *Lord Chandos Letter* (1902), a fictional letter dated 22 August 1603 from Lord Philipp Chandos to his friend Francis Bacon. In this letter Hofmannsthal gave voice to all the familiar doubts and insecurities of Viennese culture at the turn-of the-century.

Lord Chandos, still only twenty-six years old, attempts to explain his literary silence of the last two years by showing "what is inside me – a freak, a foible, a mental illness, if you like".[26] Chandos looks back with envy on his early works and his previous youthful, unbounded optimism. He reminisces about a trip to Venice when, in a sudden revelation, he had envisaged a plan and structure in Latin prose surpassing the surroundings of the splendid Grand Piazza. Another cherished project, based on the early years of Henry VIII, inspired Chandos to "an awareness of form ... which is no longer just lending order to the material, because it permeates it, abolishes it, and creates poetry and truth all at once; a play of eternal forces, a thing as magnificent as music and algebra".[27] For Chandos, his younger self, "[t]o put it briefly ... saw all of existence as one great unity".[28] This optimism and unity was, however, now shattered:

> In brief, this is my case: I have completely lost the ability to think or speak coherently about anything at all ... Everything

---

[25] Quoted in Jacques Le Rider, *Modernity and Crises of Identity. Culture and Society in Fin-de-Siècle Vienna* (Cambridge: Polity Press), p. 49.

[26] Hugo von Hofmannsthal, *The Lord Chandos Letter and Other Writings* (1902; New York: New York Review Books, 2005), p. 118.

[27] Hofmannsthal, *Lord Chandos*, pp. 118-9.

[28] Hofmannsthal, *Lord Chandos*, p. 120.

came to pieces, the pieces broke into more pieces, and nothing could be encompassed by one idea.

Yet there is consolation and hope. Chandos revels in the trivial experiences of everyday life; a half-full watering can under a tree, the contemplation of his rat-infested cellar, a moss-covered stone. He cannot express any of this in rational language, there is only "a language in which mute things speak to me ..."[29]

Many prevailing themes come together in this short fictional letter. There is the preoccupation with mental disease. There is also a profound questioning of language and of rational thought. Indeed, the Vienna of Karl Kraus and the young Wittgenstein is often referred to as the *locus classicus* of a general "language crisis".[30] The *Lord Chandos Letter* contains strong presentiments of the famous final line in Wittgenstein's *Tractatus* – "whereof one cannot speak, thereof one must be silent". There are constant allusions to Ernst Mach's theory of subjective sensations whereby continuity of the human self is placed in doubt. Or in Mach's words, "everything is in flux; the world is without substance, it is only made up of colours, contours, sounds".[31] There is a search for the mystical – first, to find the "secret, inexhaustible wisdom" of the ages and then in an attempt to somehow recapture the lost unity of existence.[32] Above all, there is, throughout the letter, a tremendous feeling of loss and dislocation. Rationality, progress and language – indeed the very fundaments of modern life and civilisation are unstable and incoherent:

[29] Hofmannsthal, *Lord Chandos*, p. 128.
[30] Donald Daviau, "Introduction" in Donald Daviau (ed.), *Major Figures of the Turn-of-the-Century Austrian Literature* (Riverside: Ariadne Press, 1991), p. xxxv-xli. Daviau criticizes the over-emphasis on the "language crisis", especially in relation to Hofmannsthal's Chandos letter. For another viewpoint see Allan Janik and Stephen Toulmin, *Wittgenstein's Vienna* (London: Weidenfeld and Nicolson, 1973).
[31] Bertha Zuckerkandl, "Literatur und Philosophie: Hermann Bahr, Ernst Mach und Emil Zuckerkandl in Gespräch, Wien 1908" in Wunberg, p. 171.
[32] Hofmannsthal, *Lord Chandos*, p. 119 Schorske, typically, is incisive and succinct on this point. Schorske, *Fin-de-Siècle Vienna*, pp. 15-22.

> Isolated words swam about me; they turned into eyes that stared at me and into which I had to stare back, dizzying whirlpools, which spun around and around and led into the void.[33]

Hofmannsthal's Chandos has stared into the abyss. As Hermann Bahr postulated: "only Austrians have truly lived, suffered, laughed, loved, dreamt and died".[34]

In 1907, on a trip to Venice, Hofmannsthal began work on a novel which would remain in fragmentary and note form until his death in 1929. In this *Bildungsroman* Hofmannsthal recounts the eventful trip of the young protagonist, Andreas, from his privileged home in Vienna to the mysterious, dark city of Venice. The novel contains specific aspects of "lateness": a "return to the eighteenth century" and Venice as the city of desire and decline. The period setting of the novel is of vital importance; indeed it is included in the first sentence, 17 September, 1778. It is in the time of Maria Theresa and Andreas's world is the one of the lower nobility, on the fringes of the Imperial Court. The first few pages, though set in Venice, evoke the prestige and power of old Imperial Austria through a masked, threadbare Venetian gentleman who lists various distinguished Austrian noble names, inspiring Andreas with a feeling of "utmost confidence".[35] Hofmannsthal uses a similar device a few pages later when the manipulative, sly servant Gotthilf offers his services.[36] In a letter from 1917 Hofmannsthal clearly places his novel in the continuum of Austrian history:

> Although it is a purely personal story, the novel takes place in the year of the death of Maria Theresa. In that year, the hero is twenty-three; in the epilogue, in 1808-9, he is an eminent official; his son is to be a diplomat, his grandson a deputy in the Paulskirche in 1848, so that all of it looks forward to the present.[37]

---

[33] Hofmannsthal, *Lord Chandos*, p. 122.

[34] Zuckerkandl, "Literatur und Philosophie", p. 176.

[35] Hugo von Hofmannsthal, *Andreas* (1932; London: Pushkin Press, 1998), p. 13.

[36] Hofmannsthal, *Andreas*, p. 23.

[37] Quoted in Le Rider, *Modernity and Crises of Identity*, p. 100.

Andreas's voyage, the decisions he makes, mirrors those of Imperial Austria.

The eighteenth century Viennese world of Andreas is one of elegance, hierarchy and privilege. Yet shadows appear almost immediately upon Andreas's departure for Venice. The first few days start well. In Carinthia, country life, in particular the farmer's unaffected daughter Romana, exudes a feeling of simplicity and purity. Andreas's servant Gotthilf breaks this idyll by stealing horses, raping Romana and in the process disgracing Andreas in front of the respectable farmer's family. Venice, unlike sunlit Carinthia, is a dark bewildering maze of alleys, piazzas and Churches, where masks and strange encounters are commonplace. The city is inhabited by mysterious women – one is running a lottery for her virginity, another plays the role on an innocent, naïve courtesan and there are hallucinatory flashes of women throughout Andreas's dream-like, night-time wanderings. Perhaps the two women Andreas glimpses in church are the characters Maria (the lady) and Mariquita (the coquette) later fleshed out in Hofmannsthal's notes. They constitute a feminine double. Maria, on the one hand, is subtle and profound, "[h]er chief concern is the unity, the uniqueness of the soul".[38] Hofmannsthal is once again seeking an unattainable unity, here portrayed in the figure of Maria. Mariquita, on the other hand, is "all latent eroticism" a woman of separate physical details – "knee, hip, smile".[39] She is sexually deviant, a true decadent in spirit and action:

Once she sleeps with two men at the same time; she says: "Suppose I had slept with the one a day, six hours, two hours, half an hour, ten minutes after the other – well what then."[40]

At the conclusion to Hofmannsthal's notes we read: "[o]utcome of tour of Venice: he feels with horror that he can never return to the narrow life of Vienna, he has grown out of it".[41] But, in fact, he does return to Vienna and catches a fleeting glance of the world's unity:

[38] Hofmannsthal, *Andreas*, p. 130.
[39] Hofmannsthal, *Andreas*, p. 130.
[40] Hofmannsthal, *Andreas*, pp. 134-5.
[41] Hofmannsthal, *Andreas*, p. 183.

He sees the sky, small clouds over the forest, sees the beauty, is moved – but without that self-confidence on which the whole world must rest as on an emerald; — with Romana, he says to himself, it might be mine.[42]

In the end, neither the Spanish double Maria/Marquita nor the allures of Venice heal Andreas's mental crisis. His only chance would have been through the faithful Carinthian maiden Romana. Andreas also recollects with envy the healthy, courageous character of his grandfather who had come to Vienna along the Danube and made the family fortune. Life was simpler and easier then.

It is significant that in the novel Venice and Spain are figures of seduction and desire. Habsburg monarchs ruled Spain (1516-1700) and Venice (1797-1805, 1814-1866) for significant periods of time. These territorial gains proved too tempting to pass up for the acquisitive Habsburg family. Nevertheless, according to the nineteenth century Viennese journalist and historian Heinrich Friedjung, this over-extension was the source of Austria's decline. In 1877 Friedjung, a strong German nationalist and Jew, wrote a pamphlet on the internal, dualist structure of Austria-Hungary arguing that in the past the Habsburgs had asked too much from its subjects.[43] For Friedung, the Habsburgs had overestimated their strength and taken on too many tasks; the Austrian branch, for example, were simultaneously on the thrones of Germany, Austria, Italy and Hungary as well as the principal defenders of Christendom against the Islamic threat.[44] Friedjung regretted the subsuming of German national interest to dynastic ambition. The tragic consequences only became apparent after Austria's defeat in the Austro-Prussian War of 1866. Prussia now dominated Germany and Austria was cut loose from its traditional historical and cultural attachment to the larger German-speaking area, resulting in a period of relative decline. Hofmannsthal was undoubtedly aware of Friedjung's ideas which were common

---

[42] Hofmannsthal, *Andreas*, p. 183.

[43] Heinrich Friedjung, *Das Ausgleich mit Ungarn. Politische Studie über das Verhältniss Österreichs zu Ungarn und Deutschland* (Leipzig: Otto Wigand, 1877), p. 22.

[44] Freidjung, *Das Ausgleich mit Ungarn*, p. 23.

currency in post-1866 Vienna.

Around one year after the initial idea for Andreas, Hofmannsthal wrote to Richard Strauss of a Venetian comedy which could serve as the basis of an opera. It was the play *Christina's Journey Home* (1910) set (like Andreas) in the Venice of the eighteenth century and featuring the figure of Casanova (called Florindo in the play). Hofmannsthal had only ten years earlier finished another play, *The Adventurer and the Singer* (1899), based on a separate episode in Casanova's memoirs. For the Viennese of the time, Casanova proved a fascinating figure. As well as Hofmannsthal's two plays, Casanova formed the subject of two works by Arthur Schnitzler, one by Raoul Auernheimer and an extended essay by Stefan Zweig. Casanova, like his home city Venice, signified both desire and decadence; he had a powerful sexual vitality but also moral bankruptcy.

Obliged to present his Casanova comedy on the Viennese stage, Hofmannsthal spent three quiet afternoons in February 1909 drafting a scenario for an opera; the beginnings of *Der Rosenkavalier*. It would be "full of burlesque situations and characters, with lively action, pellucid almost like a pantomime".[45] Hofmannsthal was very specific about the time and place: "old Vienna under Empress Maria Theresa".[46] After a meeting in Berlin around March 1909 Strauss agreed to the project and almost immediately began work on the music. Hofmannsthal, in particular, pushed for a light-hearted, sentimental comic opera. In a letter from early in the project, Hofmannsthal advised Strauss to "think of an old-fashioned Viennese waltz, sweet yet saucy, which must pervade the whole of the last act".[47] Work progressed quickly and on 26 January 1911 *Der Rosenkavalier* was premiered in Dresden. It proved an immediate success and has retained its place in the repertory ever since.

Can *Der Rosenkavalier* be classed as a "late work"? In one respect it cannot. At the Dresden premiere Strauss was 47, Hofmannsthal 36. Strauss would continue composing until his 84th year,

---

[45] Franz Strauss, Alice Strauss, and Willi Schuh (eds.), *The Correspondence between Richard Strauss and Hugo von Hofmannsthal* (London: Collins, 1961), p. 27.
[46] Strauss, Strauss and Schuh (eds.), p. 27.
[47] Strauss, Strauss and Schuh (eds.), p. 30.

including the astonishing group of post-World War II works – the *Metamorphosis* (1945) and the *Four Last Songs* (1948) in particular exhibiting a profound sense of melancholy and farewell. Yet both Hofmannsthal and Strauss were youthful prodigies, in their early works displaying an amazing technical grasp, especially of older traditions. This familiarity and mastery of conventions is evident throughout *Rosenkavalier*. In this respect the opera does contain one element of Adorno's "late style"; namely the repeated use of conventions. Hofmannsthal in particular often looked to older works for inspiration and for *Rosenkavalier* took elements from Moliere, Beaumarchais and Louvret de Couvray along with period detail from Johann Khevenhüller-Metsch's diaries. The Italian schemers Valzacchi and Annina are stock figures from Comedia dell'Arte and there are numerous standard situations from comic theatre traditions; for example, the scene at the beginning of Act III with its trapdoors, ghosts, cross dressing and dubious claims of paternity.[48] There are also constant echoes of previous operas, especially those of Mozart, the most accomplished Austrian composer of the eighteenth century. Ochs often resembles Don Giovanni, especially in his futile pursuit of Mariandl (Octavian dressed as a chambermaid) and his coarse asides about Sophie. The Marschallin's personality, of course, was largely inspired by Figaro's Countess and this extends to the action, where the Marschallin's intervention in Act III mirrors the Countess's entry at the end of Figaro. Musically, Strauss utilises traditional forms: in Act I there is a staged aria and throughout the opera, waltzes intertwine with singing. Indeed there are even hints of operetta, a point mentioned by many contemporary critics.[49]

Hofmannsthal's and Strauss's conventions, however, do not function according to Adorno's theory. For Adorno, the relationship between conventions and subjectivity lies at the heart of "late works":

Troubled by death, the masterly hand sets free the matter it previously formed ... hence the conventions [are] no longer

---

[48] See the discussion of Hofmannsthal's sources in Alan Jefferson, *Richard Strauss "Der Rosenkavalier"* (Cambridge: Cambridge University Press, 1985), pp. 12-20.
[49] Jefferson, *Richard Strauss*, pp. 98-108.

imbued and mastered by subjectivity, but left standing. As subjectivity breaks away from the work, they are split off.[50]

In "late works" conventions stand naked, separated from subjective control — there is no reconciliation. This is not the case for *Rosenkavalier*, indeed any of Strauss's works. Said describes Strauss's style as "free of contrast and real tension, unthreatening [...] smoothly polished, technically perfect, worldly, and at ease *as music* in an entirely musical world".[51] *Rosenkavalier* was the beginning of Strauss's style as a seamless flow of music; certainly in his earlier works, especially *Salome* (1905) and *Elektra* (1909) there were jarring rhythms and harmonies. Strauss's mature works, however, is music without edges.

This calm and assurance is reinforced by the opera's eighteenth century setting; described by Said as a society of "overpowering wealth and privilege [...][of] seemingly limitless capacity for self-indulgence, amusement and luxury".[52] This is a world both abstract and universal, an artistic island. It is the harmonious, unified world which for Hofmannsthal and his generation seemed so irrecoverable. In *Rosenkavalier* Hofmannsthal and Strauss have turned away from the insecurity and despair in modern life and constructed an alternative, idealised world. For Hofmannsthal, in particular, the era of Maria Theresa is also equated with Austrian greatness. No matter if the reality of the eighteenth century was an Austria stretched to the limits by Frederick the Great's Prussia along with, at various times, France, Savoy, Saxony, Bavaria, Spain; or that aristocratic society was subjected to extra taxes, a centralised state and increased military commitments; or that the secret police were prevalent and religious intolerance widespread. Hofmannsthal's eighteenth century had no relation to reality; rather it was an aesthetic and psychological necessity. In *Ariadne auf Naxos*, also set in the Vienna of Maria Theresa, Hofmannsthal has Ariadne sing the following words:

There is one Empire where everything is pure,
It also has a name: Empire of the Dead

---

[50] Adorno, *Beethoven*, p. 125.
[51] Said, *On Late Style*, p. 46.
[52] Said, *On Late Style*, p. 39.

In the eighteenth century the Habsburgs were still heads of the Holy Roman Empire, with its roots in the universal conceptions of ancient Rome and medieval Christendom. Eighteenth century Austria was still the most powerful state in Germany. After the Austro-Prussian War of 1866 and the formation of Bismarckian Germany, Austria's situation was very different. The glory and unity of Maria Theresa's Empire was no more, but for Hofmannsthal what was more important was that it had existed or, at least, it could exist. According to Said's interpretation, in *Rosenkavalier* and later operas, by working within standard conventions and recalling an earlier age – before Wagner, before the French Revolution – both Hofmannsthal and Strauss affirmed the coherence and vitality of tradition. In the context of modernity, Said argues, this is a defiant stance.[53]

One of the important elements in "late style" is hope. Yet it is effortful and exposed. Adorno notes that:

> [...] in Beethoven's late style this hope flourished very close to the margin of renunciation, and yet is not renunciation. And I would think that this difference between resignation and renunciation is the whole secret of the pieces.[54]

In *Der Rosenkavalier* the Marschallin renounces her claim on Octavian but will continue to take lovers.

The young Hofmannsthal saw no reason to resolve the dilemma of modern man. The poet revelled in visions of death and silent grandeur. In 1894 Hofmannsthal wrote in his diary:

> What a desperate (or exasperated) generation of artists we are, swimming through the noisy and confused tempest of the times with the "crown of art between our teeth". ... How surprising it is that we should be perhaps the last thinking men in Vienna, the last complete men, with a soul, while after us there will perhaps come a great barbarism, a Slav and Jewish world, a sensual world. Think of Vienna destroyed, her walls all fallen,

---

[53] Said, *On Late Style*, p. 47. Said has often professed admiration for traditional philology and its old world scholars such as Erich Auerbach, Leo Spitzer and Ernst Curtius.

[54] Adorno, *Beethoven*, p. 193.

the inside of her body laid bare, her wounds covered by rampant vegetation, everywhere bright green foliage, silence, lapping water, all life extinct: what a splendid outlook, a splendid vision![55]

The image could well be that of Venice – "lapping water" – rather than Vienna. Yet after facing the possibility of complete breakdown in his confessional *Lord Chandos Letter*, Hofmannsthal was determined to find some consolation, even if it meant creating it himself. He had not given up hope on mankind or on Austria. But the attempt, however courageous and profound, was at the same time light-hearted and artificial – like *Rosenkavalier*, a farce. Hofmannsthal, so representative of his generation, remained perched between degeneration and regeneration, decadence and renewal; between the Venice of Casanova and the Vienna of Maria Theresa. This tension partly explains the richness, vitality and ambiguity in Hofmannsthal's work, indeed, one could say, in all of Viennese culture standing at the crossroads of modernity.

[55] Quoted in Le Rider, *Modernity and Crises of Identity*, p. 13.

A Cabinet of Uncertainties:
the Marianne North Gallery as Hybrid Space

Lynne Howarth
University of Nottingham

Every person interested in horticulture, botany, and art will join with Sir Joseph Hooker in feeling "grateful" to Miss North for her fortitude as a traveler, her talent and industry as an artist, and her liberality and public spirit.[1]

The purpose built gallery at the Royal Botanical Gardens in Kew, which continues to house the paintings of the nineteenth-century botanical painter Marianne North, was opened to the public on 7 June 1882. *The Gardeners' Chronicle* reviewed the opening on Saturday 10 June 1882, stating that "there are in this unique collection no less than 627 oil paintings of plants, and landscapes in which plants form a prominent part".[2] *The Chronicle* also went on to report that under the letter "A" in the gallery's accompanying catalogue that there were "no fewer than 103 entries of plant names, so that it is no exaggeration to say that a visit to this collection of pictures [...] gives the visitor an opportunity of acquiring a good idea of the natural vegetation of the greater part of the world".[3] North's importance as a botanist was also acknowledged with the range of flora she had discovered being listed alongside a statement that "there are several handsome and remarkable plants here represented that are at present unknown both in gardens and herbaria".[4] Indeed, at the time of the gallery's opening some of the species painted by North had not yet been named by science.

The Gallery itself was described by *The Chronicle,* as "an adjunct to a botanical garden" and "unique"; North's paintings being compared favourably to other forms of botanical illustration, which, it was argued, "seldom or never give life-like representations of plant life, habit, and natural surroundings".

---

[1] *The Gardeners' Chronicle*, 10 June 1882, pp. 764.

[2] *The Gardeners' Chronicle*, p. 763.

[3] *The Gardeners' Chronicle*, p. 763.

[4] *The Gardeners' Chronicle*, p. 764.

North's work was also described in the same article as a "noble collection of oil-colour sketches", which had been, "dashed off with such bold and truthful drawing and colouring that the fruits themselves seem to be before the visitor in a living state".[5] Moreover, it was considered that the verisimilitude of North's work was such that not only would botanists be able to name nearly all the plants represented, but zoologists and entomologists would be able to identify the numerous birds, animals and insects that were featured alongside them.

The hanging of the Gallery was arranged geographically, in the following order: Tenerife, Brazil, Jamaica, the United States, California, Ceylon, India (with a series of sacred plants of the Hindus), Singapore, Borneo, Java, Japan, New Zealand, and Australia — the Australian and New Zealand sketches being the most recent additions. The numerous paintings of trees by North were also accompanied by actual examples — as *The Gardener's Chronicle* attested: "a great number of timber trees are portrayed, and the whole dado of the room is made up of polished specimens of the woods derived from the trees sketched above".[6] The reporter then went on to state that "each example of wood is named" and that the catalogue to the gallery had been deliberately "cut up, framed and glazed in pages, and hung under the pictures, so that every person who desires to see and learn may do so [...] without the expenditure of a penny".[7] Visitors to the gallery were therefore left under no illusions as to its intended purpose as focus for scientific education.

The gallery itself, which was designed by Mr. James Fergusson, F.R.S., was, however, reported somewhat negatively by *The Gardener's Chronicle* to be "really much too small for the pictures to be properly seen in – a room two or three times the size of the present one is required".[8] The same report was equally critical of North's chosen décor, stating as it did that "[w]e were not quite pleased with the big and heavy classic ornament under the cornice, and we think the shiny black frames are too strong in colour".[9] As

---

[5] *The Gardeners' Chronicle*, p. 763.
[6] *The Gardeners' Chronicle*, p. 764.
[7] *The Gardeners' Chronicle*, p. 764.
[8] *The Gardeners' Chronicle*, p. 764.
[9] *The Gardeners' Chronicle*, p. 764.

the writer of the article also stated, in the centre of the gallery's main room mounted on a metallic table was a large map of the world illustrating the distribution of vegetation; "a most elaborate and highly – finished water-colour drawing by Mr. Trelawney Saunders". North's future intention of placing "a similar but larger map painted upon the ceiling", was perceived to be an "excellent idea" to be carried out at some point in the future.[10]

North's decision to offer her paintings for permanent exhibition at Kew was almost certainly influenced by visits there as a younger woman with her father, Frederick North: a Member of Parliament, whose many distinguished friends included Sir William Hooker, the then director of the gardens. Because of this connection, North is likely to have had direct access to the Museum of Economic Botany at Kew whose construction Hooker had overseen during the late eighteen-forties. This museum, which accommodated a collection of textiles, drugs, gums, dyes and timbers accumulated by Hooker over quarter of a century or more, was originally housed in an existing brick building situated in the Royal Kitchen Garden at Kew, the central room of which had been modified by the architect Decimus Burton to include a skylight and a gallery as well as furnishings with glazed wall and table cases. As such, the museum was perceived by Hooker himself "as complementing the living collections in the Gardens by exhibiting examples of products derived from them".[11] In 1857 the museum was moved to a new location at the eastern end of the pond at Kew, at which time "the original arrangement of exhibits by commodities" was replaced by "a taxonomic grouping" with objects displayed in "glazed mahogany cabinets on the three floors of what was now referred to as museum 1", where, "flower paintings, engravings and portraits" were also hung. Further donations were made to the museum from time to time, including items from international exhibitions, such as one held at Kensington in 1862, which "added an outstanding collection of colonial timbers" to the display.[12] The arrangement of the gallery built to house North's paintings at Kew some twenty-five years

---

[10] *The Gardeners' Chronicle*, p. 764.

[11] Ray Desmond, *The History of the Royal Botanic Gardens Kew* (London: Harvill Press, 1995), p. 191.

[12] Desmond, *The History of the Royal Botanic Gardens Kew*, p. 193.

later, with its atrium and first floor gallery housing actual plant specimens alongside examples of botanical illustration, is in many ways similar to that of Hooker's museum. Indeed, colour photographs of Hooker's museum from the nineteen-sixties when it was still in existence (it has since been dismantled) reveal a space very close in size and design to the North gallery, with trestle tables in the centre of the room comparable in layout to the seating arrangements and framed paintings set out in the middle of the North gallery. In addition, the same photographs show the use by Hooker of black Japanned frames similar in design to those used by North. The collection of woods contained by the North gallery would also appear to echo the collection of woods by Hooker. North's presentation of the woods was, however — as previously indicated – incorporated into her gallery's design not as a grouping of specimens but in the architectural form of a dado. Nevertheless, it might be argued that while North's gallery also placed far greater emphasis on the painted image than Hooker's museum, North may well have looked towards the latter as a ready exemplar of legitimate, high-minded scientific display.

The intended function of the North gallery simply as a site of scientific exposition is, however, far from clear. Documentation of events leading to its construction reveal continuing concerns over North's wish that it should afford visitors access to refreshments. As correspondence related to the construction of the North gallery shows, while the parliamentary lords responsible for the conduct of public spaces in London were inclined, in the wake of the public success of the Great Exhibition of 1851 to think in terms of the broader welfare of society, Joseph Hooker and the board of governors at Kew almost certainly influenced their decision to oppose North's request because of institutional concerns about the need to protect Kew's standing as a centre of serious scientific study.[13] A letter from Hooker, dated 7 November 1879, indicates, that at some stage he may well have had candid words with North on the subject. Here Hooker writes that, "Miss. North has frankly and unconditionally withdrawn her proposition as to the sale of refreshments in her proposed gallery", pointing out that she had not taken into consideration, the scale of persons taking advantage

[13] The Royal Botanical Gardens Kew, Archive and Library Letters (MN/2/3: North Gallery 1882 – 1938 MF).

of the refreshment rooms and declaring, "[h]er view was simple that she w.d [sic] like to be able to obtain tea for herself and such as her friends as being particularly interested in her work w.d [sic] occasionally make a prolonged visit to her gallery".[14]

Hooker's objections to the serving of refreshments at the North Gallery were almost certainly influenced by earlier problems he had faced during his time as director at Kew. Matters of this sort concerning the relationship between Kew and the public often included dialogue with Parliament. On one occasion, at least, Hooker was accused of "despotic behaviour" in this regard. Sir Trevor Lawrence a Member of Parliament for Burford Lodge, Dorking, and a "plantsman" was concerned about the habitual problem of Kew's opening times to the public, a problem that would continually plague Hooker during his directorship. Lawrence announced that Hooker was "full of what I cannot but call inveterate prejudice on this question". Lawrence apparently "deplored" a reference by Hooker to "a swarm of filthy children and women of the lowest class [who] invaded the Gardens" as well as the "serious charge against the people that they resorted to the woods for immoral purposes in great numbers".[15]

The implicit blurring by North of the boundary between the internal space of her proposed gallery and the exterior Gardens at Kew through her wish to provide refereshments was clearly problematic not only for Hooker, but also for the other Board Members at Kew, who were evidently worried about the erosion of any rational distinction between the realms of scientific enterprise and recreation. The potential use of the North gallery as a public tea room was almost certainly perceived to be problematic also because it echoed what many on the board at Kew saw as a previous violation of the sanctity of science in favour of entertainment by the Great Exhibition of 1851. The board's objection, to the North Gallery's intended refreshments, was not simply about the refreshments themselves, but to how they threatened to alter the definition of the space from one of scientific enlightenment to something similar to the Crystal Palace, where high-minded display had been made to take on an

[14]The Royal Botanical Gardens Kew, Archive and Library letters (MN/2/3: North Gallery 1882 – 1938 MF).

[15] Desmond, *The History of the Royal Botanic Gardens Kew*, pp. 237-238.

additional role as public spectacle. Through the unfolding of modernity, Kew had — as the correspondence surrounding the construction of the North gallery amply demonstrates — become what might now be referred to as a "contested space". Joseph Hooker's objections, to the North Gallery's intended refreshments, was not simply about the refreshments themselves, but how they threatened to alter the definition of the space from one of scientific enlightenment to something similar to the Crystal Palace, where high–minded display was made to take on an additional role as public spectacle.

In addition, the North gallery can also be understood to have challenged any clear distinction that might have been drawn between its role as a focus for secular-scientific display and as a source of artistic-aesthetic pleasure. While from the outside the gallery is largely unadorned, mixing as it does somewhat obscure traces of ancient Greek and a more obvious colonialist architecture,[16] internally it is far more ornate and highly eclectic in its layering of stylistic influences. The floral frieze, surrounding the interior of the gallery, is very much "Greek" in influence. The frieze also contains an emblem, of North's initials, influenced perhaps by "the Ionic order" which was itself based "on orientalising patterns of flower and scroll".[17] As Carol Duncan has indicated, from the eighteenth century through to the mid–twentieth Century, museum spaces were often deliberately designed to resemble Greek and neo-classical Renaissance architecture. Moreover, they have, she suggests, "always been compared to older ceremonial monuments such as Palaces or temples". Consequently, argues Duncan, museums can be understood to have functioned not simply within the "realm of secular knowledge" as the focus for "the scientific and humanistic disciplines practiced in them – conservation, art history, archaeology", and as "preservers of the community's official cultural memory", but, in addition, as places of ritualised,

---

[16] Anthony Huxley ed., *A Vision of Eden: The Life and Work of Marianne North* (Richmond, Surrey: Royal Botanical Gardens Kew 1993), p. 7.
[17] John Boardman, Jasper Griffin and Oswyn Murray eds, *The Oxford History of the Classical World* (Oxford: Oxford University Press, 1995), p. 284.

enervating experience.[18] As Duncan admits, ritual — which is associated with religious practices and likened to "magic, real or symbolic sacrifices" and "miraculous transformations, or overpowering changes of consciousness" — may appear to "bear little resemblance to the contemplation and learning that [...] museums are supposed to foster".[19] It does, however, she suggests, have a continuing relationship within a secular society with aesthetic experience and its persistent associations with notions of individual transcendence, subjective transformation and changes of consciousness. Indeed, as she points out, the anthropologist Victor Turner, whose ideas of liminality (that is to say quasi-religious experience) were developed from data gathered from non-Western cultures, also recognised strong affinities between his use of those ideas and institutionalised "western notions of the aesthetic experience".[20] The North Gallery with its conspicuous embodiment of the accepted nineteenth century conception of the museum as a surrogate temple, arguably presents itself, therefore, alongside other similar gallery and museum spaces of the time, as a hybrid space; one that announces itself simultaneously and uncertainly both as a site of aesthetic contemplation and objective scientific revelation.[21]

Moreover, North's paintings, could be interpreted in Duncan's terms as exploiting their latent liminality as "art" as a means whereby "individuals could step back from the practical concerns and social relations of everyday life and look at themselves and their world – or at least some aspect of it – with different thoughts and feelings". According to Duncan, the enactment of "ritual" is "thought to have a purpose, and end[...] [i]t is seen as transformative, conferring or renewing identity or purifying or restoring order in the self or to the world through sacrifice, ordeal, or enlightenment". By extension, Duncan argues,the beneficial outcomes of visiting a gallery space are that upon leaving "visitors come away with a feeling of having been spiritually nourished or restored". To which extent, the staging of the North gallery may

---

[18] Carol Duncan, *Civilizing Rituals: Inside Public Art Museums* (Oxford: Routledge 1995), pp. 7-8.
[19] Duncan, *Civilizing Rituals*, p. 8.
[20] Duncan, *Civilizing Rituals*, p. 11.
[21] Duncan, *Civilizing Rituals*, p. 8.

be seen to act not just as an opportunity for viewers to survey the world in microcosm, but also to enter into a transformative engagement with North's representation of it, both through her paintings and the accompanying map and guide.

With its allusions to sacred Greek architecture the gallery therefore provides a site for the historical journeying of "pilgrims", following a structured narrative route from the exterior verandah to the interior gallery. Moreover, it offers points of sacred "contemplation" prompting its pilgrims to imaginatively re-live the sacred story of North's journeys. According to Duncan, the enactment of "ritual" is "thought to have a purpose, and end[...] [i]t is seen as transformative, conferring or renewing identity or purifying or restoring order in the self or to the world through sacrifice, ordeal, or enlightenment". By extension, Duncan argues, the beneficial outcomes of visiting a gallery space are that upon leaving "visitors come away with a feeling of having been spiritually nourished or restored".[22] It is perhaps unsurprising, then, that since its opening the North gallery has become something of a shrine to those who find pleasure and inspiration in North's paintings. Many visitors over the years have bestowed personal markings within the gallery space. According to Jonathan Farley, currently senior conservator in the library and archives at Kew, the perspex which currently covers the gallery's painted door surrounds is there specifically to protect them from human finger grease. In the past, continual touching of the surround on either side of the doors darkened the paintings so much that it was thought by many to have worn the images away completely. However, when the area was cleaned during restoration in 1981 it was found only to have been discoloured. According to Farley, the bust of North set inside the gallery is also covered in a greasy, soot-like substance, which was found, yet again, to have been human finger grease, left behind by what might be seen as the ritualistic touching of a sacred effigy (the bust within the North gallery space is, in fact, a likeness of her niece Katherine Furse who modeled for the bust because she was the one female relative that resembled North as a younger, more "ideal", subject).[23] If the

[22] Duncan, *Civilizing Rituals*, p. 12-13.
[23] Interview with Jonathan Farley, the Royal Botanical Gardens Kew, February 2007.

Gallery had been allowed to serve refreshments, there would also arguably have been an informal enactment of the Eucharist, with tea, coffee and biscuits taking the place of bread and wine.

To complicate matters further, Fergusson and North's choices in the design of the outside of the gallery, could also be perceived as a reminder of what Duncan has called "a pre–Christian civic realm"; one whose "classical porticos, rotundas, and other features of Greco – Roman architecture could [be used to] signal a firm, adherence to Enlightenment values".[24] In short, between the inside and the outside of the gallery it is possible to perceive a shift in the significance of North and Ferguson's appropriation of the antique from the rational to the liminal and back again.

The hanging of the paintings at the North gallery is, perhaps, equally problematic in this regard. On entering the main display space the visitor is confronted by an overwhelming array of botanical and topographical paintings that completely cover the walls of the lower gallery from the height of the dado to the under part of the running gallery; each of which has been individually framed by a black, Japanned surround and placed securely behind leaded glass. The viewer is thus presented with something akin to a huge cabinet of curiosities that permanently fixes the images it holds like so many butterflies in a case. Moreover, at the time of the gallery's opening in 1882, not only was the North gallery's display of paintings perceived by the artist herself to have been more or less complete, it also effectively protected North's paintings from the interference of Kew's Botanists, who until very recently were allowed to alter and over-score botanical illustrations and paintings in the collection of the gardens in the service of scientific exactness.[25] Nevertheless, despite this apparent fixity, the actual experience of viewing the images at first-hand within the North gallery is a less than stable one. The sheer scale of the imagery held up to view is such that the gaze of the viewer is constantly deflected from one image to the next. What purports, on the face of it, to be a searching and exhaustive representation of the natural world consequently becomes, through the act of viewing, a sublime engagement with baffling illimitability.

[24] Duncan, *Civilizing Rituals*, p. 10.
[25] Interview with Marilyn Ward, the Royal Botanical Gardens, Kew, February 2007.

North's Gallery therefore provides us with an uncertain framework within which to view her work that is neither a wholly secular-scientific space, nor wholly an art gallery, but that is also, in a sense, both a secular-scientific space and an art gallery at one and the same time; a framework which engenders a tension not only within the space of display itself, but also within the numerous paintings it contains, which can be viewed by turns as scientific documents and as works of art. What is more, this tension between the liminal and the scientific can be seen to have been amplified by the gallery's contested relationship to the external space of the gardens at Kew. Something which, as we have already seen, clearly forced North's friend, Joseph Hooker, to police the boundaries of his own personal rational-secular view of that space.

Added to all of which, it is also possible to view the construction of the North gallery as contributing to the uncertainty of these limits through its self-conscious doubling of the external world of the garden. To visit the North gallery, visitors are first obliged to make their way through the surrounding gardens — visiting, perhaps, the extensive collection of exotic plants in the "Palm" and "Temperate" houses and lingering on the wrought iron benches on the gallery's veranda on the way — before entering the gallery through a small entrance hall after which they are confronted, beyond a set of double-doors, with the inner sanctum of the gallery space itself. In this way, the gallery's interior presents us both with an "interior" record of North's travels and a seamless adjunct to the "exterior" world of the gardens beyond. In addition, the design of the internal space with its tiled Minton style floors and garden benches, accompanied by black wooden framing stands containing further paintings by North, would appear to have been designed to further blur the boundary between interior and exterior by imitating the layout of the verandah surrounding the gallery façade with its latticed iron benches placed upon a Minton styled floor. Farley has even suggested that there was no practical or aesthetic "necessity to have [the iron benches] in the gallery", but that North made direct use of them to duplicate the experience of contemplating the outer world of the garden within the gallery itself. Consequently, North can be understood to have attempted to present visitors with an experience analogous to the gardens surrounding the gallery, but one which ultimately draws on their proximity to underwrite the capacity of her work to offer an expansive and transporting vision of a wider world beyond.

The original benches in the gallery space were replaced by Sir Arthur Hill in the 1930s. At approximately, the same time, the interior floor tiles were removed, and replaced by fashionable "ruboleum". Farley believes that this was to get away from a then unfashionable Victoriana and a desire to modernise the gallery as much as possible. It had been suggested at the time that leather sofas could be placed in the gallery to emulate the interior of the National Gallery in London, but this idea never came into fruition. The removal of the tiled floor, "ripped part of the psychology [out] of the gallery" according to Farley; thereby compromising North's intention to allow visitors the simultaneous experience of an exterior and interior world. Current conservation proposals for the gallery include the restoration of the tiled floor as well as facsimiles of the original benches.[26]

Today as part of the modern process of restoration we peel away material archeologically in the hope of revealing something of the truth. In stately homes we pare back layers of paint to expose the past's real, and not presumed, tastes in colour and pattern. In alignment with this tendency Farley has removed a section of wood next to the studio room in the gallery to expose the original, dusty pink colour of the wall and skirting board. This can be seen to marry with the cornice painted by North, which is in parts discoloured due to previous restoration work — its fading blamed on the use of non-leaded paint, which Farley believes allowed the previous sections painted by North to remain stronger in colour. The wall, Farley declared, had not seen the light of day since 1886, when North completed the placing of the woods within her dado design. Farley has also discovered that the stencil paintings presently running around the upstairs verandah were completed in the 1980s, replacing original works by North now in storage at Kew. In completing the current restoration of the North gallery Farley does not want to encroach upon the fabric unduly, declaring that he will keep technology in the background — his creative solutions to the problems presented, giving the gallery "the best of both worlds" (Victorian and contemporary) while

---

[26] Interview with Jonathan Farley, February 2007.

retaining a room prior to the aestheticism of the 1890s. Fluorescent lights will be removed, replaced by fibre optics. Hanging globe lights, which were originally used by North, will also be returned. The paintings themselves are to be re- hung. The conservation of the gallery structure means that, the pictures must be taken off the walls and returned using a new hanging and locking system that allows for a gap between the walls and the pictures so that the building may breathe. Fergusson's under floor heating system will also go. Farley believes it has caused an imbalance on the cold walls that has warped the exotic woods. A new ventilator system will therefore be installed that will, it is hoped, stop spores from settling on the walls following the discovery of dry rot in the gallery in 1981. Farley believes that the under floor system was yet another design compromise for the gallery. It allowed, he suggests, Fergusson a justification to apply a classical "Roman" heating system which has not benefited the gallery's structure. Fergusson's use of "cloistral lighting" has, however, benefited the paintings, and was the correct choice according to Farley, even though it creates a hard reflection on the glazing of the gallery's paintings.[27]

In returning to the North gallery's original layout another repressed significance is also, arguably brought to the fore. The gallery's pre–aestheticist order places its contents in a setting that strongly echoes those specifically designed for ancient ritual. It therefore also carries with it the traces of another complicating characteristic of the space: namely its bringing together of a supposedly objective, de-aestheticised form of representation – the botanical illustration – with nineteenth century notions of the transformative powers of art.

[27] Interview with Jonathan Farley, February 2007.

Photographs

The interior of the Marianne North Gallery at the Royal Botanic Gardens, Kew. (Reproduced with the kind permission of the Director and the Board of Trustees, Royal Botanic Gardens, Kew.)

The interior of Joseph Hooker's Museum of Economic Botany at the Royal Botanic Gardens, Kew, now dismantled. (Reproduced with the kind permission of the Director and the Board of Trustees, Royal Botanic Gardens, Kew.)

Inclining towards Reversion: Gu Dexin's *2007.04.14*

Paul Gladston
University of Nottingham

Current thinking on the subject of contemporary Chinese visual art is marked by a significant divergence of views. While many writers, both from within China and elsewhere, continue to analyse contemporary Chinese visual art with direct reference to Western critical theory — not least, because of that art's conspicuous appropriation of techniques from the Western avant-gardes and post avant-gardes – a number of others, so far all of them Chinese, have begun to question the efficacy of such an approach on the grounds that it effaces the insistent "Chineseness" (the specifically "Chinese" cultural identity) of contemporary Chinese visual art. As a result, there would now appear to be an abrupt division between writers, including the Chinese curator and critic, Hou Hanru,[1] whose understanding of contemporary Chinese visual art remains strongly wedded to Western poststructuralist notions of cultural performativity and hybridity, and others, amongst them the renowned Chinese curator, critic and art historian, Gao Minglu, who think of the cultural significance of contemporary Chinese visual art in considerably more certain terms.

As one might expect, the thinking behind this resistance to Western critical discourses stems from an insistence that contemporary Chinese visual art differs markedly from its Western counterpart both in terms of significance and historical direction, and, moreover, that these differences are the direct result of sharply diverging conditions of production existing either side of the China-West cultural divide. According to Gao Minglu, for example, Western critical practices such as those associated with "deconstruction" and "feminism" are simply incompatible with any attempt to arrive at meaningful understanding of contemporary Chinese visual art since they have emerged in relation to a trajectory of Western socio-cultural and economic development that differs markedly from that surrounding China's

---

[1]See Hou Hanru, *On the Mid Ground* (Hong Kong: Timezone 8, 2002).

current, and arguably somewhat belated, entry into modernity.[2] Indeed, other Chinese writers have attempted to give further weight to this position by arguing that contemporary Chinese visual art is more directly engaged with the immediate circumstances of its production and reception than contemporary Western visual art. Consider here, for example the Chinese curator Zhao Shulin's recent contention that contemporary Chinese artists have explicitly rejected not only Western modernist notions of progressive specialisation, but also a Western postmodernist attempt to dislocate visual art from the formative conditions of its production and reception; a double negation which, he argues has endowed contemporary Chinese visual art with "special aesthetic and sociological meaning".[3]

From a Western standpoint this sets up what is, of course, a now all too familiar notional opposition between, on the one hand, poststructuralist re-conceptions of "history" as an illimitable and irretrievably complex series of unfolding (socio-cultural) re-contextualisations and re-motivations, and, on the other, persistent sociologically inflected attempts to explicate the significance of artworks with direct reference to the conditions of their production. As one half of this supposed opposition, "poststructuralists" are usually understood to hold the view that sociological readings are unduly simplistic in their prioritisation of the conditions of production as the prime mover of cultural meanings, while, as the other half, "social historians" are understood to reject poststructuralist readings of art on the grounds that they demonstrate an insufficient grasp of the formative conditions under which cultural production takes place and are therefore, in effect, ahistorical. The difficulty with this notional antimony is that the division of "poststructuralist" and "sociological" positions upon which it rests is by no means as clear-cut as the rather crude caricature above suggests. As the

---

[2] Gao Minglu, "Who is Pounding The Wall? A Response to Paul Gladston's 'Writing On The Wall – (and Entry Gate): A Critical Response to Recent Curatorial Meditations on the "Chineseness" of Contemporary Chinese Visual Art'" , *Yishu: Journal of Contemporary Chinese Art* 6, 2 (June 2007), pp. 106-115.
[3] Zhao Shulin, "Social Art" in Zhao Shulin (ed.), *Shu Yong: Made in China* (Shanghai: Eastlink Gallery, 2007), p. 11.

present author has argued elsewhere in response to Gao Minglu's assertions about the inappropriateness of using Western critical discourses to address the significance of contemporary Chinese art, poststructuralist conceptions of historical narration do not, despite the neo-formalism of a great deal of deconstructive analysis, specifically preclude a close attention to the historical conditions within which works of art are both produced and received.[4] Indeed, poststructuralism's persistent problematisation of the imposition of categorical boundaries points directly towards an ineluctable state of interaction between art and the life-world and, therefore, the necessity in analysing the cultural significance of works of art for a close and continuing attention to the circumstances surrounding their production and reception. Consequently, the divergence between sociological and poststructuralist readings of history can be understood to relate not to the difference between a close attention to the conditions of production on the one hand and an outright rejection of that attention on the other, but instead to the specific issue of the latter's problematisation of the causal priority accorded to the conditions of production by the former. While socially deterministic readings are based on the synchronic notion that the prevailing conditions at the time of the initial production of a work of art are – in the final analysis — *the* prime mover of its cultural significance, poststructuralist readings would tend towards the co-ordinated synchronic/diachronic view that the cultural significance of an artwork arises unstably in relation to an unfolding interaction between that artwork, the initial conditions of its production and the changing circumstances of its reception over time, and, what is more, as Hal Foster has averred, that cultural meaning is not historically cumulative (sedimentary), but instead open to a

---

[4] See Paul Gladston, "Writing On The Wall – (and Entry Gate): A Critical Response to Recent Curatorial Meditations on the 'Chineseness' of Contemporary Chinese Visual Art" in Yishu : Journal of Contemporary Chinese Art 6, 1 (March 2007), pp. 26-33. See also Paul Gladston, "(More Writing on) The Wall: Reshaping (Gao Minglu's Vision of) Contemporary Chinese Art", *Yishu: Journal of Contemporary Chinese Art* 6, 3 (September 2007), pp.103-110.

continual process of recontextualisation and remotivation.[5]

To return to the specific question of the diverging views surrounding the cultural significance of contemporary Chinese visual art, it could therefore be averred from a poststructuralist standpoint that the deterministic position adopted by Gao and others is not only unduly limiting in its (paradoxically, somewhat Western-rationalist) assertions about the special status of the conditions of production in China (arguing, as they do, that those conditions are somehow exempted from an entanglement with a spatially wider and temporally extended history of interaction and exchange with others), but also sweeping in its exclusion of Western poststructuralist approaches to reading as entirely ahistorical. What is overlooked here in particular is not only poststructuralism's acceptance of the necessity for close attention to the historical conditions of production and reception as part of readings which see art as the locus for a dynamic interaction and exchange between spatio-temporally differing, though interrelated, social and cultural settings, but also, in the specific case of Derridean deconstruction, an explicit acceptance that poststructuralist thinking and practice is itself the product of a certain configuration of historical circumstances (texts and con-texts) and that all discourses, including its own are continually open to the possibility of recontextualisation and remotivation in the face of changing conditions of time and place. In which regard, poststructuralist approaches to the reading of contemporary Chinese visual art could be understood not as an attempt to violently reduce the radical alterity of that art, as seen from a Western point of view, to sameness, but instead, in relation to Emmanuel Levinas's conception of "first-philosophy", as an ethically motivated sacrifice of one's own self contained sense of identity to an open, face-to-face, dialogue with otherness (a sacrifice that the likes of Gao would seem – "in the final analysis" — to be unwilling to make).

Arguably what, then, emerges here is the possibility — beyond the false dichotomy of an absolute opposition between sociological and poststructuralist readings – of an approach to the interpretation of contemporary Chinese visual art, similar in

[5] See Hal Foster, *Return of the Real: the Avant-Garde at the End of the Century* (Cambridge Mass and London: The MIT Press, 1996).

outlook to Pierre Bourdieu's conceptualisation of the field of cultural production, that rejects the singularity of both immanent (that is to say formalistic) and socially deterministic approaches to historical interpretation because of the insistent need, as Bourdieu himself has argued, "to do all these things at the same time".[6]

One possible point of departure for a renewed attention to contemporary Chinese art as a locus of dynamic interaction and exchange between spatio-temporally differing, though interrelated, social and cultural contexts, as the present author has also averred in relation to Gao's version of contemporary Chinese art history, is what might be perceived as a certain resonance between the traditional Chinese Daoist notion of "reversion" or *Fan*, where differences — as figured by the still culturally pervasive Chinese-Daoist conception of *Yin-Yang* — are held in a perpetual state of dynamic change and reciprocation with one another, and the paradoxical dialectics immanent to Jacques Derrida's conceptualisation of *différance* and "trace-structure". While it would be presumptious and, indeed, unsustainable to assume the direct compatibility of these positions – principally because of a slippage between the conventional Chinese notion that it is possible for unity to arise out of a continuing, non-synthetic reciprocation between opposites, and the insistent and often violent eschewal of totality which characterises the theory and practice of deconstruction – nevertheless both would appear to share in an aversion to the possibility of any final transcendence from one sharply defined state of being to another (or from states of being to non-being, for that matter).[7] Any discussion of this possible point of interaction and exchange is therefore almost certainly far from straightforward, alighting as it does on tantalisingly comparable though ultimately irreconcilable positions and, moreover positions whose studied non-rationality would seem to lead inexorably to rather cryptic forms of explication. As a result, it is almost certainly the case that writing on or around this subject will require protracted negotiation with a view to the emergence of

[6] Pierre Bourdieu, Matthew Adamson (trans.), *In Other Words: Essays towards Reflexive Sociology* (Stanford CA: Stanford University Press, 1990), p. 147.

[7] See Jacques Derrida, Peggy Kamuf (trans.), *Specters of Marx* (New York and London: Routledge, 1994).

a provisional lexicon notionally adequate to its uncertainties and slippages. The remainder of this essay is, despite the difficulties inherent in a negotiation of this sort, an attempt to initiate the construction of such a lexicon through the interpretation of an installation by the contemporary Chinese artist, Gu Dexin.[8]

Gu Dexin's *2007.04.14*

As anyone familiar with the Shanghai Gallery of Art will be aware, it is a venue that continues to present significant challenges for the artists who are invited to show there. Although the gallery is for the most part an unadorned "white cube" of the sort to be found in many major cities across the world, it also has two permanent architectural features which intervene powerfully in the assumed neutrality of the space. One is an atrium bounded by substantial geometric columns faced with green marble to the left as one enters the gallery that cuts through the stories above in such a way that the resulting void narrows progressively to give a false, though still vertiginous, sense of quasi-Piranesian vastness. The other is a series of windows ranged along the far wall of the gallery that affords the visitor a truly spectacular view of the Huangpu River and the metropolitan skyline of Pudong; a view which in Western terms at least, along with that opened up by the gallery's atrium, is arguably nothing short of sublime. For artists exhibiting at the gallery there is, therefore, a persistent necessity to find some means by which these insistent architectural features and their overwhelming sensory impact can either be successfully down-played (negated) or incorporated into some sort of critical dialogue with the work on display.

In Gu Dexin's solo exhibition at the gallery, entitled *2005.03.05*, the artist chose to engage with this inescapable architectural problematic in, what was then, a characteristically challenging fashion by mounting a minor retrospective of sorts involving

---

[8] The reading of Gu Dexin's *2007.04.14* that appears here is a revised version of a critical review first published on the web-site of *Yishu, The Journal of Contemporary Chinese Art* (**www.yishujournal.com**) in May 2007.

numerous objects and images culled largely from earlier installations and artworks. These included huge piles of rotting fruit (some of which served to partially obscure the outside view of the Shanghai Bund), nine chests of refrigerated pigs brains, a series of framed photographic images of meat in the process of being rubbed between the forefinger and thumb of a disembodied hand, a colossal metal flag pole laid out aimlessly along the floor, and a pair of empty red plinths (one occupying the centre of the gallery's atrium). As David Chan has indicated, Gu Dexin's installation could therefore be interpreted as engaging with its setting in two ways: first, by imposing a sense of combinatory excess analogous to the gallery's own evocation of sensory overload; and second, through the incorporation of "empty" or "natural" objects — the plinths and the flag pole, and the rotting fruit respectively — as means of undermining, by turns, the artificially staged conceits of the gallery's atrium and the accelerated "hyperreality" of the urban scene outside. The combined effect of all of which, according to Chan, was a "deconstructive" intervention not only upon un-reflexive attitudes to the Westernised institutional consecration of contemporary Chinese visual art — as staged by the potentially remotivational juxtaposition of what might be seen as a deliberate evocation of the postmodernist sublime alongside the supposed "emptiness", "naturalness" and "blandness" of a more traditional Chinese aesthetic[9] — but in addition China's official policy of unstinting economic "progress" — whose overwhelming sensory impact in the form the Pudong skyline was presumably to be seen from a Western poststructuralist point of view as having been supplanted by the assertion of moral reason implicit in the analogous sublimity of Gu Dexin's installation.[10]

Like its predecessor, Gu Dexin's more recent installation at the Shanghai Gallery of Art, *2007.04.14*, also pivoted inescapably on a problematic encounter between the work on display and the architecturally framed visions of the infinite which lend the gallery

---

[9] For an extended discussion of the blandness of traditional Chinese art, see François Jullien, *In Praise of Blandness: Proceeding from Chinese Thought and Aesthetics* (New York: Zone Books, 2004), pp. 35-39..
[10] David Chan, "Gu Dexin 2005.03.05" in Cherie Liern *et al.* (eds.), *Shanghai Gallery of Art 2005* (Shanghai; Shanghai Gallery of Art, 2006), pp. 34-36.

its distinct sense of place. This time, however, the viewer was no longer faced by the multiple piling up of objects and images that had competed for attention at the artist's previous show. Instead, s/he was faced by two newly installed architectural features: a specially constructed incline – vaguely reminiscent of Vito Acconci's *Seedbed* (1972)- whose limits were continuous with those of the gallery's usual floor space and which rose from the base of the wall nearest the entrance to join neatly with the lower edge of the windows at the far end of the gallery; and, a shallow, progressively deepening trough at the base of the gallery's atrium which emerged from the opening left behind by the incline as it intersected with the outside edges of the atrium's columns. Moreover, the viewer was also presented with two further and readily discernible elaborations on this interventionist architectural thematic: first, that the incline had been completely covered by concrete slabs, manhole covers, and drains in imitation of the dusty surface of a Chinese urban pavement; and second, that scattered randomly across a floor of bright blue resin at the base of the trough were to be found countless life-size models of fruit flies whose artificial wings sparkled with the reflected glare of the gallery's electric lights. On close inspection the viewer may also have noted that behind the grills of the installation's drain covers were numerous plastic maggots suspended inertly and somewhat obscurely in small pools of red resin.

The first impression of *2007.04.14* was therefore, by comparison with Gu Dexin's earlier installation at the Shanghai Gallery of Art, *2005.03.05*, one of a calculated restraint (an impression given added weight by the pristine cleanliness of the simulated pavement which was very much at odds with our everyday experience of its actual urban counterpart); so much so, in fact, that the aesthetic impact of the work would appear on this occasion to have been self-consciously subordinated to the forceful sensory impact of its surroundings. Indeed, the sheer insistence of the gallery's arguably sublime internal and external theatricality, which continued to draw the gaze of the viewer in a most insistent manner, detracted from the visual immediacy of Gu Dexin's work to such an extent that it may only have been through very close and prolonged looking that its staging of a relationship between the openly displayed simulacra of flies and those of the partially hidden maggots was finally revealed.

As such, this staging suggests almost inevitable comparisons with Damien Hirst's installation *A Thousand Years* (1990). While it would be invidious to use such a comparison as an index of straightforward art-historical indebtedness given the near parallel progression of Damien Hirst's and Gu Dexin's careers as purveyors of artistic carnality, it is nevertheless possible to discern here a markedly contrasting aesthetic intertextuality between the powerful viscerality of Hirst's earlier work and the rather insipid presence of Gu Dexin's *2007.04.14*. Despite the fact that both represent the same natural process, they do so in markedly different ways: in Hirst's case through the actual presentation of a "ready-made" life-cycle of the birth and transformation of maggots along with their subsequent death as flies; and in Gu Dexin's the same as a static simulation brought about by the juxtaposition of conspicuously artificial elements. What might therefore be drawn from such a comparison is that in relation to the arguably sublime incomprehensibility of Hirst's presentation of the ineffable transition from being to non-being, Gu Dexin's installation places the same transition self-consciously under suspension (*"sous-rature"*). As a result of which, *2007.04.14* would — somewhat unexpectedly, perhaps, given Gu Dexin's preceding reputation for bloody excess — appear to have been drained of any immediate or obvious aesthetic impact leaving behind in its wake what might be described, from the locus of a Western post-Duchampian artworld, as a lingering and indefinable whiff of "anesthesia".

The potential significance of this apparently deliberate suspension of aesthetic immediacy is perhaps not too far to seek. The juxtaposition of what might be seen as Shanghai's spectacular postmodernist urban sublimity with a synthetic tableau of life and death at its most base and fetid, with the latter leeched of any possible sense of transcendence from one state to another, suggests an allegory of immanent corporeal corruption running torpidly and corrosively through the subterranean bowels of the (Westernised) Chinese "monster" city. Added to which, it might also be ventured that Gu Dexin's evident eschewal of the deconstructive supplementarity of his previous show at the Shanghai Gallery of Art – a critical strategy whose effectiveness had by then arguably already been terminally compromised in the wake of the "impossible" performativity of 9/11 — in favour of the sheer "anesthesia" of *2007.04.14* is one that points, via Yve-Alain Bois and Rosalind Krauss's reading of Georges Bataille's *informe*, to the possibility of a deliberate invocation of bathos; one where the tableau on display could be understood to mount a critique of the spectacle of contemporary Shanghai not through an analogous assault on the senses, but through an intentional act of disappointment. Hence, as Cao Weijun has argued in the curatorial notes accompanying the exhibition of 2007.04.14, it is possible to interpret Gu Dexin's installation as a staged (path)way pointing us inconclusively from the baseness of the quotidian to the transcendental heavenly light held out by the self-referentially iconic vision of contemporary Shanghai – something which, Cao avers, can be interpreted still further with reference to Nietzsche's tragic conjunction of the Dionysian and the Apollonian.[11] However, while this interpretation of 2007.04.14 is consistent with the current trajectory of Western theory, I would like to argue here that it is subject to qualification when considered closely in relation to the actual phenomenological experience of Gu Dexin's work *in situ*. The construction of Gu Dexin's installation was in the end just too precise, its forms just too "good" to fully disappoint the viewer. Consequently, it was not at all clear that the view of the Pudong skyline which formed the backdrop to the installation could be read, as Cao Weijun suggests, unequivocally as a desired heavenly state from which the corporeal viewer was to be perpetually disbarred. Indeed, the internal and external visions of illimitability incorporated by the gallery against which Gu Dexin's work might be seen to rail could also be envisaged as having imported their own problematic traces of artificiality. To which extent *2007.04.14* may be interpreted as insufficiently rigorous in both its conception and execution to act as a persuasive source of critical bathos.

Seen from the locus of another cultural positioning, that of a traditional Chinese Daoist aesthetic, Gu Dexin's installation can, however, be read somewhat differently and, perhaps, more convincingly. As previously suggested, the non-rational notion characteristic of Daoism that conceives of the possibility of differing, though reciprocal states is one that can be understood to

[11] Cao Weijun, curatorial notes accompanying the exhibition of *2007.04.14* (Shanghai: The Shanghai Gallery of Art, 2007).

lead not — as is usually considered to be the case in relation to the quasi-analogous Derridean conception of *différance* — to a persistent sense of anti-foundational incompleteness, but also to the possibility of some sort of spatio-temporally open-ended rapprochement between opposites, not least in relation to the foundational difference between Heaven and Earth (hence, amongst other things, the Chinese tradition of shielding the exposed bodies of the dead from the rain in fear that still immanent souls might experience the rather unpleasant sensation of getting wet).[12] Indeed, seen through the lens of a Daoist "metaphysical" tradition, the relative insipidity of the "corporeal" may also be thought of as impinging persistently on the "heavenly" – and *vice versa* — through a dynamic process of "reversion" (*Fan*) considered immanent to the seminal pairing of opposites, *Yin-Yang*. A process that, as Wang Keping has indicated, can be understood to reveal both "the state of being opposite" and "the state of transformation and change" through which "things are inclined to reverse to their opposites".[13] Consequently, *2007.04.14* can be read somewhat against the grain of Cao Weijun's (rather Westernised) view of its staging not as the locus of a stalled movement of transition from one ontological state to another – such an interpretation seems, in any case, far too deeply rooted, in this context at least, in the (post)modern art gallery's indubitable grounding in the sacramental (Eucharistic) rituals of Western Christianity – but as one where any absolute distinction between Heaven and Earth is qualified by a possible state of harmonious reciprocity between the two. At stake here, then, is the notion that Gu Dexin's apparent "reversion" from deconstructive sublimity did not result simply in a work that could neither imaginatively undermine the spectacle presented by its object of approbation, nor trump that spectacle through a deliberate moment of bathetic failure (arguably, a de-basing form of "deconstructive" practice),

---

[12] For some further thoughts on the possibility of *rapprochement* in relation to the theory and practice of deconstruction see Gladston, Paul, *Art History after Deconstruction* (Auckland; Magnolia Books, 2005). Also see Mark Rosenthal's informative discussion of "intervention" and "rapprochement" in Rosenthal, Mark, *Understanding Installation Art: from Duchamp to Holzer* (New York: Prestel, 2003), pp. 61-89.

[13] Wang Keping, *The Classic of the Dao: a New Investigation* (Beijing, Foreign Languages Press, 1998), p. 8.

but one which attempted to open up a (critical) space wherein there is from the outset no absolutely binding notion of a transcendental ideal in relation to which the rudeness of the present corporeal world would always be considered a shortfall. To which extent the work might still be considered as a commentary on the strategic artificiality and political/intellectual inconsistency of the motivational desires ignited by China's ruling Communist party amongst the country's people.

Put further, there is here arguably, on the one hand, as Craig Clunas has averred, amidst the complex and extended genealogy of Chinese cultural thought and action, an ambient divergence from seminal Western notions "of the ideal and unchanging forms of things, present in some superior realm of transcendence" that by extension overturns a conventional Western privileging of ""being", the unchanging, the constant, over "becoming", the changing, the situation in flux".,[14] and, on the other, a sense in which that eschewal of absolute being – as figured in relation to the conceptualisation of *Yin-Yang* — is nevertheless to be understood as having the potential to lead not simply to the irreconcilable differences and fractures of Derridean post-structuralism, but also to an abiding sense of reciprocity between opposites. In which regard, any conception of Gu Dexin's *2007.04.14* as yet another internationalised variation on the now well trammeled thematic path of Western (post)avant-gardist deconstruction is arguably open to qualification. While the work may carry the traces of a persistent appropriation of Western idioms with what is arguably an attendant postmodernist sense of disappointment, it can also be argued that it re-orientates those idioms (most notably through what might be seen as its recessive non-action) towards another, rather more reassuring and harmonious, "way", that of the "inexhaustible *Dao*" – an "Orientation" which may well, of course, to some remain unconscionably beyond the pale as yet another form of metaphysical delusion, but which to others is nevertheless the very cultural air they live and breathe and, what is more, a historically sustaining position of critical resistance to overweening (political) authority.

[14] Craig Clunas, "What about Chinese art?" in Catherine King (ed.), *Views of Difference: Different views of Art* (New Haven and London: Yale University Press, 1999), p. 126.

CULTURE, SOCIETY AND THE SELF

The Uses of East German Autobiography
since the End of the GDR

Roger Woods
University of Nottingham

Since the demise of the German Democratic Republic in 1989/90, East Germans have produced a flood of autobiographical writing. Literary figures such as Hermann Kant, Günter de Bruyn and Günter Kunert have written full-blown autobiographies.[1] Leading politicians including Erich Honecker, Günter Mittag and Kurt Hager have given their version of what they were trying to achieve in the GDR in lengthy memoirs,[2] and opposition figures who were imprisoned in the GDR such as Walter Janka have felt compelled to publish autobiographical material "in order to set the record straight".[3]

A great body of related work has also emerged in the same period: Annett Gröschner's interviews with an older generation of

---

[1] Hermann Kant, *Abspann: Erinnerung an meine Gegenwart* (Berlin and Weimar: Aufbau, 1991); Günter de Bruyn, *Vierzig Jahre. Ein Lebensbericht* (Frankfurt aM: Fischer, 1996); Günter de Bruyn, *Zwischenbilanz: Eine Jugend in Berlin* (Frankfurt aM: Fischer, 1992); Günter Kunert, *Erwachsenenspiele: Erinnerungen* (Munich: dtv, 1999). See also Günter de Bruyn's reflective essay on the issues surrounding autobiographical writing: *Das erzählte Ich: Über Wahrheit und Dichtung in der Autobiographie* (Frankfurt aM: Fischer, 1995). For details of further literary autobiographies since the Wende and an analysis of their significance see Dennis Tate, "The End of Autobiography? The older generation of East German authors take stock", in Martin Kane (ed.), *Legacies and Identities: East and West German Responses to Unification* (Oxford: Peter Lang, 2002), pp. 11-26.

[2] Erich Honecker, *Moabiter Notizen, Letztes schriftliches Zeugnis und Gesprächsprotokolle vom BRD-Besuch 1987 aus dem persönlichen Besitz Erich Honeckers* (Berlin: edition ost, 1994); Günter Mittag, *Um jeden Preis* (Berlin and Weimar: Aufbau, 1991); Kurt Hager, *Erinnerungen* (Leipzig: Faber u. Faber, 1996).

[3] Walter Janka, *Schwierigkeiten mit der Wahrheit* (Reinbek bei Hamburg: Rowohlt, 1989), p. 17; Wolfgang Harich, *Ahnenpaß. Versuch einer Autobiographie*, ed. Thomas Grimm (Berlin: Schwarzkopf und Schwarzkopf, 1999).

East Berliners, *Jeder hat sein Stück Berlin gekriegt* (Everyone got their Piece of Berlin), illustrates the full range of political awareness of ordinary citizens in the GDR,[4] while Olaf Georg Klein's semi-fictional autobiographical sketches based on interviews probes the issues of individual responsibility and guilt.[5] In the academic world sociological and historical studies that take accounts by ordinary people as their starting point reflect a growing interest in the GDR as viewed through the eyes of individuals.[6]

The following analysis takes a broad definition of autobiography that has emerged from discussions of the genre over the past two decades, looking not just at literary autobiography but also memoirs and interview material. The aim is to demonstrate how autobiography and related sources reveal a complexity and subtlety of experience that can deepen our understanding of life in East Germany.

The case for autobiography in general has been made by Gabriele Jancke who argues that reading autobiographical texts has changed her view of history:

> After reading several hundred such [autobiographical] texts I can no longer imagine any event, process, or structure without actors who can be named; and talk of "society" or "culture" — referring to a particular time or space – seems highly questionable to me. Autobiographical texts, especially when one can study a large number of them from a particular sphere, present such a variety of perspectives that approaches based on generalisation and anonymity lose their credibility. Whether a society is experienced as the same by minorities and by majorities, by intellectuals and by the uneducated, by women and by men – the question has still to be answered.[7]

---

[4] Annett Gröschner, *Jeder hat sein Stück Berlin gekriegt: Geschichten vom Prenzlauer Berg* (Reinbek: Rowohlt Taschenbuch Verlag, 1998).

[5] Olaf Georg Klein, *Plötzlich war alles ganz anders: Deutsche Lebenswege im Umbruch* (Cologne: Kiepenheuer and Witsch, 1994).

[6] Dieter Geulen, "Typische Sozialisationsverläufe in der DDR: Einige qualitative Befunde über vier Generationen", *Aus Politik und Zeitgeschichte*, 25 June 1993, 37-44; Lutz Niethammer, Alexander von Plato, Dorothee Wierling, *Die volkseigene Erfahrung* (Berlin: Rowohlt, 1991).

[7] Gabriele Jancke, *Autobiographie als soziale Praxis* (Cologne, Weimar,

Jancke's point about multiple perspectives tends to work against the construction of generalisations, and, although her point is not made with reference to the GDR, it is a useful corrective to much public debate after the end of the GDR: early re-assessments of the GDR were marked by the preoccupation with locating responsibility for forty years of socialism, and these reassessments often explicitly or implicitly separated out the population into perpetrators and victims.

At the level of historical interpretation it has been suggested that the GDR was primarily a product of political interests and only secondarily a "social entity": "East German society owed many of its basic characteristics to the establishment of a particular political regime, and indeed one which in principle was not willing to grant autonomy to any area of society". East German society, it has been argued, was totally controlled by the state, and to this extent it was a "shut down" society.[8]

If this is true there seems little point in delving into East Germany's social history. Yet research soon established that interpretative models of the GDR based on a simple division into perpetrators and victims or on total control did not do justice to a more complex reality. In his highly acclaimed study of East Germany, *Die Ostdeustchen: Kunde von einem verlorenen Land* (The East Germans: Information from a Lost Land) Wolfgang Engler writes: "Dismissive terms such as 'unjust state' and 'command economy' are just as incapable of explaining the East German experience as the grand terms 'totalitarianism', 'rule of violence' and 'dictatorship'".[9] Empirical research into milieus in East Germany in fact tended to undermine the image of a monolithic GDR in which people either supported or opposed the system. Political culture, everyday life in the GDR was clearly complex and varied, and this research confirmed the need for an understanding which took into account how individuals lived their lives.[10]

Vienna: Boehlau, 2002), p. vii.

[8] The position is summarised by Corey Ross, *The East German Dictatorship: Problems and Perspectives in the Interpretation of the GDR* (London: Arnold, 2002), pp. 45-8.

[9] Wolfgang Engler, *Die Ostdeutschen: Kunde von einem verlorenen Land* (Berlin: Aufbau, 2000), p. 9.

[10] See Thomas Meyer, "Gleichzeitiges und Ungleichzeitiges in der

Wolfgang Engler suggested a further reason for concerning oneself with the individual when he applied the concept of individuation to Eastern European societies. In the case of Western societies, the concept suggests that individuals are enabled or required to construct and arrange their lives for themselves.[11] Although the whole structure of a society based on state socialism appeared **to** many to demonstrate the impossibility and the irrelevance of individuation, Engler traces an "emancipation from dictated ways of behaving and a cultural liberation of people, even in state socialism".[12] In the Eastern European context, then, individuation refers to the liberation from life patterns which are fixed by authoritarian systems. Engler summarises the situation of many GDR citizens: "The way people behaved, and the way people related to each other and to institutions were always the result of two logic systems – the logic of dominance of a system over people and the logic of independently generated biographies".[13] Engler gives an example of what this looked like in the GDR in his comments on East German youth in the 1980s:

> At that same time [around 1987] many young people had turned their backs on the state system and found their place in subcultures. At this level readings, exhibitions, concerts, discussions, and all kinds of events took place without the involvement of any official bodies. Unlike the two preceding decades the seventies and eighties were not producing "collective novels of development", but rather successful novels of becoming a person in one's own right.[14]

---

politischen Kultur in Ost- und Westdeutschland", in Michael Müller, Wolfgang Thierse (eds), *Deutsche Ansichten: Die Republik im Übergang* (Bonn: Dietz, 1992), pp. 25-40.

[11] See Ulrich Beck, *Die Erfindung des Politischen* (Frankfut aM: Suhrkamp, 1993), p. 150.

[12] Wolfgang Engler, *Die ungewollte Moderne: Ost-West-Passagen* (Frankfurt aM, Suhrkamp, 1995), p. 31-4.

[13] Engler, *Die ungewollte Moderne*, p. 77.

[14] Wolfgang Engler, *Die Ostdeutschen*, p. 166. Engler also sees the increasing significance of the individual reflected in GDR sociology of the later 1980s, with studies of the individual, ways of life, everyday life, and leisure time articulating a broad cultural shift.

These reflections on the scope for the individual to construct his or her own life in the GDR suggest that there would be some point in looking at individuals, and they mesh with an unease about trying to get to grips with the GDR past by dealing exclusively with structures and groups. Such approaches, it is argued, do not grasp the full complexity of how individuals lived their lives in the GDR. Thomas Lindenberger thus argues for "everyday history to act as a counterbalance to social history that in the case of state socialism is in danger of turning out to be the same as the history of political institutions".[15]

The political and academic stages thus seem set for more studies at the level of the individual, and an abundance of autobiographical material is available. Yet working with autobiographical sources is not entirely straightforward: they often claim to have unique access to the truth in the shape of the author's own experiences, but this "truth" may not be verifiable. Indeed, there is often good reason to suppose that autobiographical truth is the product of what has been called active memory, meaning a conscious or unconscious reworking of the past for reasons located in the writer's present. This problem is particularly relevant to East German autobiography, given the "tribunal conditions"[16] in Germany after 1989, and the fact that many prominent East Germans were literally on trial. In writing their memoirs they were eager to exonerate themselves, typically by stressing their distance from the socialist regime or their impotence within that system. Even writers intent on conveying an accurate picture of their lives and times face the problem of writing long after the events they describe and therefore having to contend with a failing memory.

Anyone working with literary autobiographies also needs to bear in mind the cultural tradition of the writer as liar: Günter de Bruyn characterises his efforts at autobiography by saying that the

---

[15] Thomas Lindenberger, "Alltagsgeschichte und ihr möglicher Beitrag zu einer Gesellschaftsgeschichte der DDR", in Richard Bessel, Ralph Jessen (eds), *Die Grenzen der Diktatur: Staat und Gesellschaft in der DDR* (Göttingen: Vandenhoeck und Ruprecht, 1996), pp. 298-325.
[16] The term is Christa Wolf's: "Auf mir bestehen. Christa Wolf im Gespräch mit Günter Gaus", *neue deutsche literatur*, 41, no. 5 (May 1993), pp. 20-40.

"professional liar is practising telling the truth".[17] The subtitle for *Vierzig Jahre* (Forty Years), his second volume of autobiography, may be "Ein Lebensbericht" (A Report on my Life), but it is not meant to be taken at face value.

One can argue that research on autobiography is timely against the background of what has been described as an aversion among some historians "towards 'metanarratives' and overarching structures of interpretation".[18] Yet the contribution research on autobiography might make in this new context has been called into question, with the research being criticised as a rejection of "master narratives". Concentrating on the "local and the empiricial" means that the researcher is "less likely to have to deal with the abstractions of class or value, without which the system cannot be understood".[19]

In her discussion of the uses of autobiographies the historian Dagmar Günther confirms that they are increasingly popular sources among historians, but she contends that they are being read in an old-fashioned way, as if they were factual accounts.[20] Her example is research on the bourgeoisie that draws on bankers' autobiographies in which members of the profession portray themselves as having a strong work ethic. Günther takes this image as a reflection of the ethic defining maleness that was dominant at the time the autobiographies were written, but she warns that it may not be true. She suggests a more subtle but ultimately limited use for such accounts: they should be analysed not for their factual content but as "retrospective self-portraits".[21]

---

[17] Günter de Bruyn, *Zwischenbilanz*, p. 7

[18] Corey Ross, *The East German Dictatorship*, p. 5

[19] See the discussion of this position, which is associated with Frederic Jameson, in Jan Campbell, Janet Harbord (eds), *Temporalities, Autobiography and Everyday Life* (Manchester and New York: Manchester University Press, 2002), p. 1. Basing their argument on Walter Benjamin, Campbell and Harbord argue that autobiography is in fact never about the self as an isolated project, but about a self known through and embedded within the network of social relations that confer identity and meaning (p. 12).

[20] Dagmar Günther, "'And now for something completely different': Prolegomena zur Autobiographie als Quelle der Geschichtswissenschaft", *Historische Zeitschrift* 272, 1 (2001), pp. 25-61.

[21] Günther, pp. 37-8.

In the case of the East Germany a series of interviews conducted after the collapse of the GDR with members of the old ruling elite offers just such a set of self-portraits. Across the whole range of former Politburo members, ministers, senior economists, and newspaper editors the ritualised presentation of the elite repeats itself: they had certain privileges, but they worked hard, taking paperwork home and rarely making full use of their annual leave entitlement. They were democrats with very little actual power, and they did their best in difficult circumstances. Party discipline and a sense of duty and responsibility were the reasons they did not resign.[22] The motives behind such self-presentation in the early 1990s are not hard to discern, and, in line with Günther's proposed alternative reading of autobiographical material in general, the interviews are best seen as an illustration of the old GDR elite's collective self-defence after Unification than as an insight into its working habits up to 1989.

Günther criticises historical research for using autobiographical sources as "providers of facts", and for reading them in a simplistic way in order to confirm a theory or for reading them in a literal and highly selective way.[23] Magnus Brechtken similarly criticises the habit of taking memoirs at face value and overlooking the complex issue of their validity as sources.[24] This criticism is often accompanied by a growing tendency among readers of autobiographies to stress their fictional dimension.[25] In this connection Dagmar Günther contrasts the approach of literary critics and historians, arguing that the former work on the texts and the latter with them: literary critics make the form of autobiography the object of study while historians use autobiographies for their referential value.[26]

What is overlooked, according to critics of referential readings of autobiography, is an analysis of how the life story is told; the value of autobiographies lies less in their content than in their role

---

[22] Brigitte Zimmermann, Hans-Dieter Schütt, *Ohnmacht. DDR-Funktionäre sagen aus* (Berlin: Verlag Neues Leben, 1992).
[23] Günther, pp. 38-45.
[24] Magnus Brechtken, "Einleitung", in *Politische Memoiren in deutscher und britischer Perspektive* (Munich: K.G.Saur, 2005), pp. 9-42.
[25] Brechtken, p. 19.
[26] Günther, p. 59.

as "communicative acts".[27] Günther poses the questions that flow from this more complex view of autobiographical texts:

> Is the individual story told as an account of the self, as a group account, or as the history of other people? How is the life interpreted: as self-assertion, as a life determined by the external factors of circumstance or fate? What is the connection between the individual's story and the historical period? How are private stories and public events linked? What interpretative models frame the life story that is told?[28]

The second half of this analysis examines some examples of East German autobiography since 1989 against the background of such questions and the theoretical discussions about what kind of society the GDR was.

The first example addresses the question of what representative status autobiographies might have by looking at *Schwierigkeiten mit der Wahrheit* (Difficulties with the Truth), a short autobiographical text by Walter Janka, the reformist head of Aufbau Verlag in the fifties who was imprisoned in 1957 for counter-revolutionary activities. Wolfgang Engler sees two typical figures in GDR art of the 1960s: the "partisan" and the "functionary". He counts Walter Janka as a partisan, and he summarises the characteristics of the partisan as follows:

> The partisan always has the same key experiences and memories – the First World War, soldiers and crippled men returning home, the fight for a socialist German republic and the defeat, the Nazi dictatorship, concentration camp or prison, resistance or exile. And the partisan always draws the same conclusions for his life under socialism, he always ranks his own judgement above any external voice, decisive action and willingness to take a risk above pathos and ritual; and he does this so consistently that he sometimes becomes a thorough nuisance, the living bad conscience of his compliant and more disciplined contemporaries who become functionaries.[29]

[27] Günther, p. 49.

[28] Günther, p. 51.

[29] Wolfgang Engler, *Die Ostdeutschen*, p. 118.

Engler quotes from Janka's other volume of autobiography, *Spuren eines Lebens* (Traces of a Life),[30] on how he always acted independently and took responsibility for his actions. Engler comments that this is a fundamental and typical attitude which he also finds, for example, in the autobiography of Walter Markov, a communist who formed a small resistance group to the Nazis at Bonn University. Markov was imprisoned by the Nazis and expelled from the SED in 1951 for his Titoist views.[31] Engler's assessment of Janka is supported by Wolfgang Harich, his fellow reformer who was arrested with Janka in 1956. Harich describes how Janka was not intimidated by the Central Committee and was contemptuous of any bureaucrats who got in his way.[32] Engler thus uses autobiographical material to start constructing a typology based on shared experience, political attitudes, and actions, and contemporary sources suggest that this typology has some validity.

How far can one take this typology? When Janka is in trouble with the State Security he describes the response of his acquaintances. He goes to see Helene Weigel, Brecht's widow, and finds that, unlike other prominent people who pretend to be unaware of what is happening or simply cannot think what to say or do, Weigel is well informed. Janka says this had also been the case with Brecht, and it was not primarily because Brecht had friends everywhere who fed him information. Rather it was because he (and Weigel) had the "courage to be informed".[33] This response contrasts with the experience of Wolfgang Harich's mother after Harich is arrested. She goes to see Harich's boss, Fritz Erpenbeck, who says, according to Harich's mother, that he cannot do anything because he does not know what the issues are.[34] Janka goes on to describe his trial at which even well informed acquaintances do not speak up on his behalf.[35]

---

30 Walter Janka, *Spuren eines Lebens* (Berlin: Rowohlt, 1991).

31 In his own autobiography, *Zwiesprache mit dem Jahrhundert*, Markow also separates the comrades into partisans and functionaries. Quoted by Engler, *Die Ostdeutschen*, p. 119.

32 Wolfgang Harich, *Keine Schwierigkeiten mit der Wahrheit* (Berlin: Dietz, 1993), pp. 31-2.

33 Janka, *Schwierigkeiten mit der Wahrheit*, p. 61.

34 Janka, *Schwierigkeiten mit der Wahrheit*, p. 53.

35 Janka, *Schwierigkeiten mit der Wahrheit*, p. 90.

This autobiographical account does not have to be taken at face value to be of value: even if some of the detail is based on hearsay, it gives the reader an insight into the oppressive atmosphere of the time, the frequency with which people faced moral dilemmas and the variety of ways they found of responding to these dilemmas. The account also suggests that Engler's typology is too tightly drawn since it does not allow for the different actions of figures with some partisan characteristics and attitudes. On the other hand there is clearly more to be gained from reading Janka's autobiographical work than Dagmar Günther's "retrospective self-portraits". What emerges from the detail of Janka's and other individuals' lives expressed in autobiography is not so much a clear-cut typology of groups but a broad typology of group experience and milieu.

In Janka's case we gain an insight into the experiences and milieu of critical intellectuals in times of political upheaval in the Eastern bloc, and one can trace the same basic patterns in other autobiographical texts from the post-*Wende* period. Günter de Bruyn, for example, was no committed socialist, yet his description of the intellectual atmosphere in the early years of the GDR's existence echoes Janka's account of how different colleagues adopted different strategies of knowing and not knowing in their dealings with the state. In *Vierzig Jahre* de Bruyn discusses the reasons for the lack of truthfulness of his first book, *Der Hohlweg* (The Ravine, 1963). Anyone wanting to write about the war and post-war years had to lie, he explains. He knows more now than he did at the time of writing, but even then nothing was completely unknown to him. However, he felt at the time that it was better to keep what he knew to himself, so he omitted it from his novel.[36] These and other autobiographical texts certainly show individuals at very different points on Dagmar Günther's spectrum between self-assertion and a life determined by external factors, but they also show a striking consistency in their portrayal of the context of intellectual life in the GDR.

The next set of autobiographical texts explores the scope for individuals to make moral choices in the GDR, and it illustrates the importance of paying particular attention to how

[36] Günter de Bruyn, *Vierzig Jahre*, p. 117.

autobiography is written.

In his autobiography, *Erwachsenenspiele* (Games for Adults), Günter Kunert gives an account of his experience at a writers' course soon after 1945 where splits emerge between the ideological hardliners on the one side and Kunert, Erich Loest, Heiner Müller and Horst Bienek on the other. The organisers conclude that Loest and Kunert do not take the course seriously enough and require them to engage in self-criticism before the assembled group. Kunert calls this self-criticism a subjugation ritual and regards it as a challenge to his acting abilities. He puts on a show of regret even though he finds the process nauseating and regards the hardliners with contempt. Kunert is sure in his own mind that he has retained his integrity and, unlike most others, not capitulated to those in authority.[37] This autobiographical self-image is called into question, however, through a comparison with Günter de Bruyn's account of a similar situation in *Vierzig Jahre*. De Bruyn describes here how he trained as a librarian in East Berlin after the war and wrote essays that followed the Party line on books he had not even read. He justifies this approach to his studies by saying he is defeating those in power with their own weapons, and it "seems" to him that he is preserving his own intellectual freedom in the process. The verb "seems" indicates uncertainty, however, and this is confirmed when he goes on to write of his teacher that she may have seen through his show of conformism, but this will not have bothered her greatly since even the appearance of conformism was a sign of real subjugation.[38]

De Bruyn's autobiographical account of his life in the GDR is characterised by a complex ambigiuity that is at odds with Kunert's more self-assured tone. At one point he refers with obvious distaste to the Schriftstellerverband (Writers' Union) as "the heavily ideological writers' headquarters",[39] but later actually joins the Union "not least because of the social benefits".[40] His vocabulary is chosen at one level to indicate lack of choice, compulsion, and passivity: he is "launched into executive committees"; someone arranges for him to become a member of

---

[37] Günter Kunert, *Erwachsenenspiele*, pp. 140-42.
[38] Günter de Bruyn, *Vierzig Jahre*, p. 16.
[39] Günter de Bruyn, *Vierzig Jahre*, p. 90.
[40] Günter de Bruyn, *Vierzig Jahre*, p. 122.

PEN; his Western counterparts appreciate that he has to be careful what he says in the West since they understand his "forced subjugation"; he is drawn into the GDR literary scene "against his will".[41] The purpose of this vocabulary of compulsion is made clear when de Bruyn writes about the years of Nazi rule as an intellectually comfortable period since the compulsion he lived under meant that he did not need to have a bad conscience for not making any decisions or taking any actions.[42] Yet *Vierzig Jahre* is also shot through with self-doubt and self-criticism. He becomes increasingly uneasy about the ambiguity of his stance, and he calls his life a "questionable existence". He decides that he wants clarity and that an event at which he is giving a reading will be "an evening of clear front lines".[43] He wants no more compromises, but when he speaks out clearly in favour of the unofficial peace movement and there is no official rebuke he worries that "being left to get on with it" is tantamount to being embraced by the system.[44] His drive for clarity takes a further blow when he is informed he is to be awarded the National Prize, First Class in the summer of 1989. In de Bruyn's autobiography we see the idea of preserving one's integrity while appearing to conform tested to destruction.

This is a common dilemma about which one starts to see a pattern of consensus when the same issues occur in Rita Kuczynski's *Mauerblume* (Wallflower). She probes her own "questionable existence", having married into a privileged political family and working at the Institute of Philosophy in East Berlin. For many years she regarded her research on philosophical theory as her real life, as opposed to the false life which was made up of the political hoops she had to jump through in order to preserve the purity of this research. Yet she is only able to maintain this perspective by blocking out the knowledge of the other purposes of the Institute which has its research projects defined directly by the Central Committee of the SED (Socialist Unity Party). She reflects that she does not wish to know that the Institute was one

---

41 Günter de Bruyn, *Vierzig Jahre*, pp. 124, 102, 112.
42 Günter de Bruyn, *Vierzig Jahre*, p. 127.
43 Günter de Bruyn, *Vierzig Jahre*, p. 220.
44 Günter de Bruyn, *Vierzig Jahre*, pp. 250-1.

of the most important centres for legitimising SED policies,[45] and she sets out her moral dilemma:

> The question that confronted me more insistently from year to year was: how many concessions were necessary for the sake of "pure theory". How much did I have to lie, pretend, in order to preserve that little free space where my so-called pure research beyond all ideological noise was possible? [...] So I played the game: conforming, not conforming, conforming by not conforming in order to create free space for myself and to be able to leave everything just as it was. Engaging in pseudo-activities in order to create an impression of political commitment [...] It was years before I realised that I was well on the way to using myself up with these tactical games and compromises and stifling my creativity.[46]

These extracts are taken from the autobiographies of writers whose lives took different directions. De Bruyn stayed in the GDR until and after its demise, Rita Kuczynski spent time in the West but was also in the GDR in 1989, and Kunert left for the West in 1979. Although they responded differently to the pressures of life in the GDR, these pressures are described in decidedly similar terms from one writer to the next. A pattern of consensus about the intellectual atmosphere emerges, and this pattern tells a more complex and subtle story than is offered by models of the GDR that deal in stark contrasts of conformism or dissent.

The above analysis suggests that one can move away from reading autobiographical texts for facts. But it also suggests that if one takes into account their internal tensions, revealed not least in how they are written, and the ways in which autobiographies can interact and have a cumulative effect, one can find more in the texts than retrospective self-portraits that might at best be read for a glimpse into the social context and mentality of the authors at the time of writing. For these texts have something to say that is relevant to the discussions among historians about what kind of society the GDR was. Any model of a totally controlled or "shut down" society does not fit well with the tensions surrounding

<hr>

[45] Rita Kuczynski, *Mauerblume* (Munich: Claassen, 1999), pp. 111-13.
[46] Rita Kuczynski, *Mauerblume*, p. 145.

issues of personal responsibility in the autobiographies we have looked at. These tensions may not be obvious, but they are clearly present once the reader has grasped the complex structures of the texts. The collective message of these autobiographies supports Engler's view that East Germans lived with two logic systems – the logic of dominance of a system over people and the logic of independently generated biographies. Collectively these autobiographies are also a complex set of sources that show how lives were constructed within these two systems.

Reviewing the Social:
Bringing "Playing" Into the Everyday

Lili Hernández
University of Nottingham Ningbo, China

> *An unexamined life is not worth living*
> *- Socrates*

The review of social life discussed in this paper attempts to offer an alternative way of analysing the everyday. Such a review emerges from the social and the macro and reaches into the quotidian and the micro aspects of everyday life. My departure point is common to that of Lefebvre's critique of everyday life. In his words, "many men [...] do not know their own lives very well, or know them inadequately [...] In particular, they have an inadequate knowledge of their needs and their own fundamental attitudes; they express them badly, they delude themselves about their needs and aspirations except for the most general and the most basic ones".[1] For the purposes of this review, I borrow Lefebvre's notion of *critique* and I transform it into a *review*. My choice of words responds to two main reasons. First, a problem of usage: the verb *criticise,* once neutral between praise and censure, is now frequently, used in a negative way. Second, a *review* suggests the idea of *going back and seeing again,* which implies to see the everyday analytically and retrospectively with an eye to transformation. Taking on board the Socratic concern for the examination of our lives, the need for a review of everyday life is suggested here. My ideas are supported on Berger and Luckman's social constructionism of and in authors of the field of the everyday such as Lefebvre and Benjamin. Furthermore, in an attempt to avoid falling into abstractions, definitions and generalisations which deny the very essence of the everyday, my own ethnography is made part of the methodology of analysis. Such an approach is based on a tradition of thought which allows for the anecdotal, the autobiographical and the personal to emerge as part of the study of everyday life (as put forward by writers such

---

[1] Henri Lefebvre, *Critique of Everyday Life*, trans. John Moore (London: Verso, 1991), vol.1, p. 94.

as Meaghan Morris, Nancy Miller, Mellisa Gregg and Sherryl Kleinman).

The idea that inspires this review is the conception of the everyday as a field for creativity and play. I conceive of everyday life as a play where withdrawal into a reality of its own can create the conditions to experiment and try things out in a playful nonetheless real manner. As such, individuals become alternatively authors, actors and spectators of the drama of the everyday.

Theorists who prioritise creativity, singularity and resistance in everyday life often underestimate the role of the social in the shaping of the everyday (de Certeau, Highmore). This responds partly to the fact that such approaches emerged as a reaction against discourses inclined to encapsulate the everyday into abstraction, definitions and generalisations. The present review agrees with such approaches in their refusal to consider everyday life as self-evident and taken for granted, advocating the recovery of creativity and resistance as quintessential to the everyday. Nevertheless, it acknowledges too the relevance of the social as a force that impinges on the everyday. Berger and Luckmann's notions are relevant to support such an idea, as they suggest, we "apprehend the reality of everyday life as an ordered reality".[2] In other words, whether we like it or not, the social world acts as external and coercive force that confronts the individual. This does not imply the denial of the individuals' ability to create the world but the understanding of our place within such given conditions.

Lefebvre's notion of alienation supports the idea of an alienating social world strange to and separated from our identities. Such a notion is helpful to understand the split of the individual between *the private man* and the man of needs. Conflicting spirits arise as the individual seeks to satisfy the *private man's* needs while at the same time he/she is brought in relation to others. In so far as those conflicting spirits coexist, the individual experiences the feeling of being separated from the self and dragged into a sense of living a life – or some aspects of a life — imposed by others. Such life does not always suit the protagonist of the play or, at any rate, the spectators.

The case of my adoption of technologies is helpful to illustrate

[2] Peter Berger and Thomas Luckmann. *The Social Construction of Reality: a Treatise in the Sociology of Knowledge* (New York: Anchor, 1967), p. 21.

this. Overall, I tend to be resistant to trends in the consumption of goods. Branded names do not appeal to me. By and large, I shop for necessity and hardly ever for pleasure. In much the same way, I have resisted the adoption of some technologies, i.e. television, which I barely watch even if I happen to have a set in front of me; a telephone landline while I was studying in England; and, the Internet, which I adopted quite late in my life. I also resisted for a long time the purchase of a mobile phone and, once I owned such device, I resisted for a long time replacing the handset though this seemed a natural step forward. My old Samsung was quite unique in that, having been broken on several occasions it could only be held together thanks to a good amount of adhesive tape. Ever more distinctive was the fact that, having lost its microphone, the handset could only be used with a hands-free set that would act as a replacement of the lost microphone. Using my mobile phone in such a bizarre way without falling into the purchase of a new handset was a form of resistance to a market economy which strongly promotes the use – and constant renewal — of technologies.

As I moved to China, to continue to resist the purchase of a mobile phone was particularly difficult. As I started a new life in a Chinese land, I was perplexed to find out that, long before I arrived in this country, my employer had already assigned me a mobile telephone number with handset included. To my surprise, purchasing a mobile phone with the network provider chosen by my university was a recommendation/requirement of my new employer for the entire staff based in this Asian country. As the deal stood, all members of staff could have the cheapest model of a mobile phone for a small amount of money, or a better model for a reasonable difference. Employees were enticed to signing up for such a contract by having the "advantage" of a short number system by which certain number of calls within the same network are, until now, allegedly "free of charge". The short number facility is, indeed, covered by a small monthly rent paid by the employee.

Though such an institutionalised system has manifold advantages, it also entails a blatant lack of privacy. Every member of staff who enrolls in this schema has access to a common electronic phonebook in which all employees' mobile numbers are displayed. The implications of such a system yet go beyond this.

Thanks to the short number facility, the use of mobile phones has become the customary way to establish contact between members of staff not only outside working hours, but also within the time frame of work at the University. Hardly ever is the office landline used at all within the confines of work at this British university based in China. As it transpires, the deal seemed quite alienating. Moreover, the freedom to choose was further reduced by the fact that whether one "was willing" to sign this ready-made contract with the university system or with an outside network, all employees were required to provide their private mobile numbers to the human resources department for further contact.

It is important not to overlook that such a domineering system of communication was put in place in an environment where most employees who work for this British university come from different countries and, overall, they are not fluent in Mandarin. This means that the mobile phone is, indeed, an important means of "survival". As language barriers are a customary occurrence in day-to-day communication, my submission to my employer's commandment was almost inevitable. As I signed the contract that was already drawn up in my name, I kept wondering if I could find a way to resist such suggestion/imposition, even while signing up for it. The obvious possibilities appeared: to keep the mobile off outside working hours, to restrict my answering of calls only to those I choose to. Nevertheless, even as I tried out such possibilities, the feeling that my freedom was considerably reduced kept coming up. Every missed call displayed in the screen of my mobile phone was a reminder of something that, sooner or later, I had to deal with. In other words, alternatives of action – and of creativity and resistance – are often limited by manifold circumstances of the everyday to which the individuals need to adjust. Implied is the fact too that there are some benefits brought by an institutionalised system such as the one provided by my employer, making choices ever more complicated. As suggested by Steve Woolgar, while the reader/user is not absolutely forced to act in a particular way, non-preferred readings or uses are more costly, that is, they require more effort and resources than the preferred ones.[3]

[3] See Maria Bakardjieva, *Internet Society: the Internet in Everyday Life.* (London: Sage, 2005), p. 21.

The fact that I was "invited" to use a mobile phone according to the terms and conditions established by my British employer in China made me feel rather alienated. My personal preference as to whether I would like to use or not a mobile phone, and how, was relinquished to signing a standard contract designed for all employees. Given my inability to speak Mandarin, I hesitated whether it was worth the time and the predicament that I would go through in order to find a suitable contract in the market, when the end result would be the same: to provide my employer with a piece of information of my personal life, restricting my privacy and my freedom.

Walter Benjamin distinguishes between experience, that which is being lived, immediate and inchoate (*Erlebnis*) and, experience as this acquires social meaning through reflection and evaluation (*Erfahrung*). For Benjamin communicable experience is related to the knowledge that becomes shared experience, what he calls *Erfahrung*. That is to say, reflection upon our situations of life that makes the experiences transmittable to others. In my experience of mobile use in China, *Erlebnis,* the experience of signing up for the mobile phone contract designed by my employer becomes *Erfahrung,* the event itself plus my conscious reflection of it moment by moment. In that way, I became the storyteller that Benjamin speaks about. My personal experience became a shared experience as I attempted to articulate it in terms of how new information technologies such as mobile phones can be both enhancing and alienating. In addition, I detached from the experience and I re-viewed my everyday life in the light of such an event. Though a social order was imposed on me, this could not alter my own reflections and my consciousness. Hence, within the same alienating experience, I found elements of liberation. Notwithstanding that to switch off my mobile did not liberate me, the fact that I could step aside and be conscious of my alienation did give me a sense of liberation. It did so through an awareness of the fact that I was not succumbing into the play but I was consciously playing within it. I felt powerful not by my acting upon the fixed contract but by my consciousness. At the very least, I was able to articulate such an experience and to render it for reflection, not only for me but for others to reflect upon it.

As part of the emergence, maintenance and transmission of a

social order, Berger and Luckmann address the notion of institutionalisation. The latter springs from habitualisation which refers to "any action that is repeated frequently [and that] becomes cast into a pattern".[4] Habitualisation implies that actions can be repeatedly performed with an economy of effort. Berger and Luckmann emphasise that "habitualisation makes it unnecessary for each situation to be defined anew, step by step [...] the activity to be undertaken in these situations can then be anticipated".[5] Habitualised activity opens up a space for creativity and innovation because the tension of the new is relieved and substituted instead by a sense of predictability of our own behaviours and the behaviours of others. Moreover habitualisation does not only open the space for creativity and innovation, but also for transformation. The "there he goes again" or "there we go again" that Berger and Luckmann refers to, and that, at times is experienced as a weight on us contains, within, the feeling of alienation that may lead to transformation.

Walter Benjamin's ideas of boredom are helpful to support the idea of habitualisation as a source of creativity. Benjamin sustains that "we are bored when we don't know what we are waiting for. That we do know, or think we know, is nearly always the expression of our superficiality or inattention. Boredom is the threshold of great deeds. – Now, it would be important to know: What is the dialectical antithesis to boredom?"[6] It is risky to venture an answer to such question. Nevertheless, the notion of time in modernity might be useful to propose what the antithesis of boredom might be. In the state of modernity that Zygmunt Bauman theorises about time is strongly linked to an imperative for instantaneity. Bauman's describes the attributes of what he calls *Liquid Modernity,* suggesting that while instantaneity is made the ultimate goal, time evades, flows, spills, runs out, leaks, floods, sprays and drips. To a certain extent, our busy lives inscribed within time in modernity may act as perfect antidote against boredom. My own ethnography is helpful to illustrate such a state.

I was allegedly brought up to "be successful". According to

---

[4] Berger and Luckman, *The Social Construction of Reality*, p. 53.
[5] Berger and Luckman, *The Social Construction of Reality*, p. 54.
[6] Walter Benjamin, *The Arcades Project* (Massachusetts: The Belknap Press, 1999), p. 105.

those who were in charge of my education, I was an intelligent and dynamic girl with the potential to achieve great success in life. Regardless of what this meant for my parents, relatives and teachers, for me it was no more than a burden. Ever since, and judged by particular social standards, my everyday life has frequently been described as "successful". This judgement is based on what could be regarded as a gradual achievement of certain goals: doing well at school, being fairly competent in most enterprises I embark on, having a reasonable job, having the means to increasingly acquire material goods that overall speak of "economic success" (a car, a house, the holidays here and there) enjoying an active social life, having the prospect of forming a family of my own, and so forth. Relatives, friends and acquaintances have often judged these as part of having a "successful life". However, if that was the case, it was also at the expense of my having barely any opportunity for a deeper reflection of the meaning of my life. I was caught in a battle against time. The trap of the elusiveness of time weighed over me and, the more I wished to apprehend it as I accomplished – or not — "my" goals, the more it evaded me. In the midst of this battle against time, a question kept repeatedly coming up. Is this all there is? That was the very question that triggered the need to engage in the review of my everyday life, a scrutiny of my life which further from being finalised, unfolds as I speak.

What was socially considered a successful life represented for me the challenge of dealing with an excess of practices within an evasive and ever flowing scope of time. Such an overflow of practices contributed to an antithesis of boredom, that is, there was not much time for great deeds, for reflection, or for transforming *Erlebnis* into *Erfahrung*. Furthermore, while some of my everyday practices and attitudes used to enrich my life, some others impoverished it. Amongst the former I could count reading, cooking, listening to music, being in contact with nature, listening to others' concerns and afflictions, and the like. The latter, on the other hand, were constituted by those practices in which I was required – or in any case, guided or persuaded — to behave in a particular way. Overall, the practices and attitudes that I experienced as impoverishing my life were all inscribed within a continuous, unstoppable and fast accelerating consciousness of time. Such goals were constrained by a dimension that was impossible to apprehend, that is, time in modern life. An element of velocity and speed was involved in how successful I could be at work, in achieving material goods, in using new technologies or in forming my own family. The more efficient I was, for example, at work, or at dealing with technologies, or the higher the position I could achieve in my job, the more time I needed to devote to these practices. I used to feel as if the goal that was once a few steps away increasingly receded and evaded me. The same was the case with forming my own family. There was a biological watch indicating, mercilessly, the right and only time to achieve such a goal. Overall, as I experienced the demand to act in accordance to a "successful" social standard of life, there was not much time to create an everyday of my own.

The possibility to transform such alienating circumstances of life materialised as I was aware of the alienation brought into my life by such an objective social world. This by no means suggests that by adopting the idea of alienation our actions are transformed at once. Instead what is conveyed is the notion that we can relativise the arrangements of our social reality, taking distance from such circumstances of life and embracing the idea of transition as part of the everyday. As it happens in the play, there is room for creativity when actors create and recreate their characters as part of a given script. Similarly, the possibilities for creativity emerge as our everyday lives unfold within the institutions of an objective social world.

A fundamental premise of this review is, thus, the idea of transformation. Although the influence of the social as external and coercive force is rather inescapable, what is possible to introduce into the everyday as lived by the individuals is a new perception of the social world with its institutionalised patterns. The idea of transformation implies that, within the objectivity of the social world, the arrangements of our lives are rather variable. Fixed categories exist only as part of particular perceptions of reality. If perception changes, a whole sense of transformation takes place in that which was originally perceived. This idea can be better understood with reference to Stanley Cohen and Laurie Taylor who suggest that

> [...] it is the de-mystification itself which, by allowing us to distance ourselves from the social arrangements to which we are party, gives us a sense of satisfaction with our own lot [...] the fact that we can regard with amusement the conventions of university or office life and our roles as teachers or managers, actually ensures that we remain within those conventions and these roles.[7]

Cohen and Taylor's study about the mental management of routine by prisoners in a maximum-security wing in Durham prison is very significant for a review of the everyday in that it rescues a sense of the importance of oneself as part of the ability to relativise our experiences. However, I do not agree with their assumption that to relativise our social arrangements entails "a slightly decreased sense of social commitment".[8] Instead, the recovery of the importance of oneself means apperception of such a commitment. That is to say, a new perception based in knowledge and experience, as opposed to the perceptions hitherto prevalent. In this very sense, apperception implies that the self is not completely lost while conceding to such social arrangements.

This allows me to bring into the discussion Donald Winnicott's ideas about creativity and play. According to Winnicott, to see the everyday anew requires seeing, in retrospect, the experiences that moulded particular ways of being in and looking at the world. That is to say, to relativise the social as internalised reality. According to Winnicott, creative living means to be equipped with some capacity to see the outer world both as created and in the process of being created. This makes possible to retain something personal in our interactions with the outside world. Living creatively means the ability to construct a "personal" relationship with the objects of the social world that come in the way.

Winnicott's compelling theory of transitional objects and phenomena is helpful to understand the baby's journey towards experiencing creativity. According to Winnicott, "transitional objects and phenomena – the blanket, the teddy bear, etc. — represent the original 'not-me' possession that the baby uses in

---

[7] Stanley Cohen and Laurie Taylor, *Escape Attempts: the Theory and Practice of Resistance to Everyday Life* (2nd ed.; London: Routledge, 1992), p. 56.
[8] Cohen and Taylor, *Escape Attempts*, p. 56.

his/her journey from the purely subjective to objectivity. Through the transitional object the baby starts a process of distinguishing between inner objects and external objects, between fantasy and fact, between primary creativity and perception. This early stage in development is made possible by the mother's special capacity for making adaptation to the needs of her infant, thus allowing the infant the illusion that what the infant creates really exists."[9] Winnicott argues that if the mother is able to adapt to the baby's needs, the baby has no initial appreciation of the fact that the world was there before he or she was conceived or conceived of. From this develops Winnicott's ideas of "the magic of imaginative and creative living".[10] which can be better understood through the notion of *playing*.

Playing is "always a creative experience [...] a basic form of living [...] a line between the subjective and that which is objectively perceived".[11] Winnicott emphasises that the significant moment in playing is "that at which the child surprises himself or herself".[12] Surprise takes place because of the near-withdrawal state in which playing takes place. The child who plays inhabits in its entirety an area that cannot be easily left. This would be the equivalent to an adult's concentration. However, for the playing child, the content does not matter. He dwells in a neutral zone. Winnicott claims that "it is only here, in this unintegrated state of the personality, that that which we describe as creative can appear".[13]

Berger and Luckmann address the notion of play as the turning away of the attention from the reality of everyday life. They suggest that in such way "a radical change takes place in the tension of consciousness".[14] This, precisely, makes playing an important transitional area between the subjective and the objective. Playing, indeed, facilitates the relativisation of our experiences, the turning away of the attention from our social arrangements. As it happens with the child who withdraws into

---

[9] Donald Winnicott, *Playing and Reality* (Oxon: Routledge, 2005), p. 19.

[10] Winnicott, *Playing and Reality*, p. xvi.

[11] Winnicott, *Playing and Reality*, p. 67-8.

[12] Winnicott, *Playing and Reality*, p. 68.

[13] Winnicott, *Playing and Reality*, p. 86.

[14] Berger and Luckman, *The Social Construction of Reality*, p. 26.

playing, the contents of what is being experienced do not matter all that much but only the fact that we are playing. To relieve the tension of the everyday in such a way implies a shift in consciousness. It suggests the idea of going inside and seeing the alienating aspects of our lives with a detached perception. Such a detached consciousness frees us from the tension of achieving complete success/perfection in the practices of our everyday lives. Instead it finds a middle point where creative living becomes an individual's attempt to accept external reality without too much loss of personal impulse.[15]

Berger and Luckmann address the notion of playing as a finite province of meaning inscribed within the paramount reality of everyday life. Such a province of meaning speaks of a transition between both realities: the world of playing and the world of reality. Playing as a finite province of meaning creates a new way of understanding the social world that impinges. We take refuge in that province of meaning only to come back again to the paramount reality of everyday life with renewed perception. In my own very way, the use of my sellotaped-mobile phone in England acted as a refuge for me; a turning away from the demands both of an overwhelming market economy and of a technologically driven society into a province of a meaning of my own creation.

Winnicott's theory of playing does not leave the realm of reality. Playing and reality become part of the same array of experience. Although playing brings to the fore creativity and imagination, it is not idealised. Winnicott acknowledges that playing is always liable to become frightening. This by no means undermines playing. Instead it re-asserts that playing belongs to being alive and as such it implies risks, gambles and manifold instances of trial-and-error. Transferred to the domain of the individuals within the social, this means the acceptance that there are instances of the everyday in which creative inclinations are lost in favour of social determinants as it was the case of my ready-made contract for a mobile phone in China.

Creative living implies the rescuing of our ability to surprise ourselves in our everyday experiences. The surprise can be as simple as taking a walk in an unknown but mythical part of the

---

[15] Winnicott, *Playing and Reality*, p. 46.

city, or to do so at unexpected times or with unexpected company. The surprise could as well be to find something amusing in what I have always believed I am incapable of enjoying — maybe finding the convenience of Eastern toilets, which are often a challenge for many Western women, or trying out that dish that I have never been brave enough to taste. The surprise can go so far as to detach us from the fruits of our actions, whether good or bad, whether perceived as successful or unsuccessful and, to see them only as part of the play.

Furthermore, creative living entails to amuse ourselves by laughing at the transitional character of the arrangements of our social lives. Today we feel successful because we have achieved something *good*. Tomorrow the same event might bring us further worries. We may point at someone else's mistake and, later it is our mistake which we need to look at. By the same token, the relativising of our experiences means the possibility to laugh at our perceptions because they belong only to the realm of our imperfect mind. We get annoyed by someone's performance and we believe in this behaviour as objectively belonging to that person. Surprisingly, studies in Psychology suggest that when others' behaviour triggers anger in us that behaviour is likely to be, indeed, a hidden part of ourselves that we do not like and we refuse to accept. The relativising of experience could go on and on in such an amusing way to the point of allowing boredom in our lives as an entryway for great deeds.

A review of everyday life, understood in this way implies that amid the alienating experiences in the individual's life, what creative living recovers is a thread that, as it is constantly pulled out, can provide not only a change in the ways of looking at both the inner and the outer worlds but also, a renewed way of experiencing the everyday. The search for creative living occurs both within and without, not as part of a process but instead, within endless instances of trial-and- error as part of the relativising of experience.

It is important to emphasise that the review of everyday life does not prescribe a formula for creative living. A review of everyday life speaks of transition. It implies the understanding of the social world as a field of alienation, which, at one and the same, time triggers the need for transformation. This awareness, in turn, opens the space for the unknown and the unexpected, for experimentation and play. Ultimately, a review of everyday life takes on board the Socratic concern for the examination of our lives. Though, the intricate path for such a review may better correspond with Breton's suggestion that, "perhaps life needs to be deciphered like a cryptogram",[16] an idea that brings us back into the play of the everyday.

[16] André Breton, *Nadja* (New York: Grove Press, 1999), p. 112.

Notes on Contributors

Andrew Cobbing is Lecturer in Modern History in the School of History at the University of Nottingham. He recently spent two years on secondment at the University of Nottingham Ningbo, China from 2005 to 2007. His recent publications include the co-authored *Kawada Ryokichi: Jeanie Eadie's Samurai* (Global Oriental, 2006) and three biographical essays in *Japanese Envoys in Britain* edited by Ian Nish (Global Oriental, 2007).

Armida de la Garza is Lecturer in International Communications at the University of Nottingham Ningbo, China. Her recent publications include *Mexico on Film: National Identity and International Relations* (Arena, 2006). She is currently working on a research project entitled "Transnational Cinema in Globalising Societies".

Paul Gladston is currently seconded from the School of Modern Languages and Cultures at the University Nottingham as Head of the Division of International Communications Studies and Director of the Institute of Comparative Cultural Studies at the University of Nottingham Ningbo, China. His recent publications include *Art History after Deconstruction* (Magnolia, 2005) as well as an extended critical dialogue with the curator and art historian Gao Minglu, which appeared in successive editions of *Yishu*, the international journal of contemporary Chinese art during 2007.

Germán Gil-Curiel is Lecturer in International Communications at the University of Nottingham Ningbo, China and PhD Candidate in Comparative Literature at the University of Sheffield. His research interests lie in supernatural literature and the relationship between music, literature and film.

Lili Hernández is Lecturer in International Communications at the University of Nottingham Ningbo, China. Her recent publications include *Globalisation of Information Technologies and the Exclusion of Everyday Life* (Common Ground Publishers, 2004). She was one of the organisers at the University of Nottingham Ningbo, China of the international conference *Crossing Cultural Boundaries* (2007) and is currently co-editing a book *Crossing Cultural Boundaries: Taboos and Other Issues around the Body* (Cambridge Scholars).

Nicholas Hewitt is Professor of French and Head of the Department of Cultural Studies at the University of Nottingham, where he is also Director of the Institute for Comparative Cultural Studies. He is the author of books on Henri Troyat, Louis-Ferdinand Céline, interwar "malaise" and the French literary Right, and the editor of *The Cambridge Companion to Modern French Culture*. He has published extensively on the cultural history of Montmartre and is currently working on Marseille.

Lynne Howarth is a PhD candidate at the University of Nottingham. Her research focuses on the life and work of the nineteenth-century botanical illustrator and traveller, Marianne North. Her recent publications include "Weeds as Diaspora" in Nicholas Hewitt and Dick Geary (eds.) *Diaspora(s)* (CCCP Press, 2007).

Michael Kelly is Professor of French and Head of the School of Humanities at the University of Southampton. He is also Director of the UK Subject Centre for Languages, Linguistics and Area Studies, and a Fellow of the Higher Education Academy. In these capacities he has a strong interest in the philosophy of education and in the different approaches to education in different intellectual traditions.

Jonathan Kwan is Lecturer in Modern History at the University of Nottingham and until recently was part of the International Studies Division at the University of Nottingham Ningbo, China. His main area of research is the development of Austro-German liberalism and his recent publications include "Competing Historical Narratives: Memory, Identity and Politics in Nineteenth-Century Bohemia" in Hans Henning-Hahn and Heidi Hein (eds.), *Politische Mythen im 19. und 20. Jahrhunderte in Mittel- und Osteuropa* (Marburg, 2006).

Colin Mackerras is Professor Emeritus in the Department of International Business and Asian Studies, Griffith University, Queensland, and author of many books and scholarly articles on China, especially its theatre and ethnic minorities. Among his main recent publications are *China's Ethnic Minorities and Globalisation* (Routledge-Curzon, 2003); he is the "Traditional China" section editor and a major contributor to *The Encyclopedia of Asian Theatre* (Greenwood Press, 2007).

Lúcia Nagib is Centenary Professor of World Cinemas and Director of the Centre for World Cinemas, University of Leeds. Her major research subjects are cinematic realism, New Waves and contemporary New Cinemas. She is the author of the books *Werner Herzog: Film as Reality* (Estação Liberdade), *Around the Japanese Nouvelle Vague* (Editora da Unicamp), *Born of the Ashes: The Auteur and the Individual in Oshima's Films* (Edusp), *The Brazilian Film Revival: Interviews with 90 filmmakers of the 90s* (Editora 34) *and Brazil on Screen: Cinema Novo, New Cinema, Utopia* (I.B. Tauris). She is the editor of *The New Brazilian Cinema* (I.B. Tauris), *Ozu* (Marco Zero) and *Master Mizoguchi* (Navegar).

Robert Stam is University Professor at New York University, where he teaches on the subject of French New Wave film makers. He has published widely on French literature, comparative cultural studies and Cinema including topics such as film history and film theory. His major publications include *François Truffaut and Friends: Modernism, Sexuality and Film Adaptation* (Rutgers University Press, 2006) and *Reflexivity in Film and Literature: from Don Quixote to Jean-Luc Godard* (Columbia University Press, 1985).

Roger Woods is Professor of German at the University of Nottingham and Vice-President of the University of Nottingham Ningbo, China. He researches on modern German culture and has recently completed a book *The New Right in Germany as Culture and Politics* (Macmillan, 2007). He is currently editing a volume of essays on German life writing in the Twentieth Century.